Essential GraphRAG

Get the eBook FREE!

(PDF, ePub, Kindle, and liveBook all included)

We believe that once you buy a book from us, you should be able to read it in any format we have available. To get electronic versions of this book at no additional cost to you, purchase and then register this book at the Manning website.

Go to https://www.manning.com/freebook and follow the instructions to complete your pBook registration.

That's it!
Thanks from Manning!

Essential GraphRAG

Knowledge Graph–Enhanced RAG

Tomaž Bratanič
Oskar Hane
Foreword by Paco Nathan

MANNING
Shelter Island

For online information and ordering of this and other Manning books, please visit www.manning.com. The publisher offers discounts on this book when ordered in quantity. For more information, please contact

Special Sales Department
Manning Publications Co.
20 Baldwin Road
PO Box 761
Shelter Island, NY 11964
Email: orders@manning.com

Manning Publications Co.
20 Baldwin Road
PO Box 761
Shelter Island, NY 11964

Development editor: Ian Hough
Technical editor: Arturo Geigel
Review editor: Kishor Rit
Production editor: Kathy Rossland
Copy editor: Kari Lucke
Proofreader: Katie Tennant
Technical proofreader: Jerry Kuch
Typesetter: Dennis Dalinnik
Cover designer: Marija Tudor

ISBN: 9781633436268
Printed in the United States of America

brief contents

contents

foreword

In *Essential GraphRAG*, Tomaž and Oskar demonstrate how to implement a GraphRAG system from scratch, without relying on existing frameworks. They pull back the curtain, revealing the code behind contemporary AI applications. The book covers major GraphRAG innovations through worked examples you can code and run. Exercises explore nuances and alternatives, with references to primary sources on arXiv. Starting with simple RAG patterns, chapters progress through GraphRAG techniques to agentic workflows.

By working through these coding examples, reading referenced articles, and solving exercises, you'll learn

- How RAG improves large language model accuracy by retrieving external data
- How knowledge graphs extend RAG for more structured and precise information retrieval
- How to use query rewriting techniques and strategies for embedding and document chunking, adapted for various use cases
- How to build agentic systems for complex scenarios

At every step, Tomaž and Oskar guide you on improving retrieval accuracy, structuring responses, and evaluating results, helping you understand the tradeoffs of mixing and matching approaches for your specific needs.

Ultimately, the power of AI applications doesn't come from ineffable magic but from confident, experienced builders who understand these technologies and continuously learn by doing. We've seen large language model–based applications evolve rapidly over the past eight years, with much more to come. This book provides a solid foundation for building the future.

—Paco Nathan
Senzing, Principal DevRel Engineer

preface

This book came about because we (Oskar and Tomaž) had been working together for a few years at Neo4j and kept arriving at the same thought: someone should write a book about combining knowledge graphs with retrieval-augmented generation (RAG). We figured it might as well be us. The idea wasn't born from some grand epiphany—it was just a practical realization. We'd both spent enough time with graphs, machine learning, and generative AI to see that large language models (LLMs) had real limitations, like outdated info or missing domain-specific details. Knowledge graphs seemed like an obvious way to fix that, and it wasn't that hard to put the two together.

Our backgrounds made it a natural fit. Oskar, with over 20 years as a software engineer and a decade at Neo4j, leads the generative AI engineering team, focused on helping developers build GenAI apps with graphs. Tomaž has deep experience in graph algorithms, machine learning, and LLMs, contributing to frameworks like LangChain and LlamaIndex while writing about practical LLM applications. Together, we'd already been tinkering with these ideas—extracting structured data from text, plugging it into graphs, and using it to boost RAG. It worked well enough in our day-to-day that we thought others could use it too.

The result is this book. It's not here to overcomplicate things or sell you on some revolutionary breakthrough. We wrote it because we've seen GraphRAG solve problems in a way that's practical and doable, whether you're new to this or already deep in the weeds. If you're curious about making LLMs sharper with graphs, this is our take on how to get it done. Simple as that.

acknowledgments

We'd like to thank everyone who helped make this book possible. To our colleagues at Neo4j: your insights, feedback, and shared passion for graphs and generative AI kept us on track and inspired us to dig deeper. A special nod goes to the engineering and research teams—your work laid the groundwork for many ideas in these pages.

We're grateful to the Manning team for guiding us through the process with patience and expertise. Their support turned our rough drafts into something worth reading. Special thanks go to Paco Nathan for writing the foreword to this book. Many thanks also go to technical editor Arturo Geigel for the invaluable help that he gave us. Arturo is an independent researcher from Puerto Rico who is recognized for being the inventor of Neural Trojans and currently carries out research machine learning, graph theory, and technological analysis.

Thanks also go to the reviewers who took the time to read early versions and offer sharp, constructive notes that made this book better: Abhilash Babu, Adil Patel, Avinash Tiwari, Balbir Singh, George Robert Freeman, Giampiero Granatella, Gourav Sengupta, Harpal Singh, Igor Karp, Jared Duncan, Jayesh Kapadnis, Jeremy Chen, John Montgomery, Kanak Kshetri, Kasanicova Kristina, Laurens Meulman, Mehmet Yilmaz, Michael Bateman, Najeeb Arif, Peter V. Henstock, Praveen Gupta Sanka, Rani Sharim, Ravindra Jaju, Richard Meinsen, Ronald Borman, Saravanan Muniraj, Sergio Fernández Gonzalez, Shiroshica Kulatilake, Shyam Viswanathan, Sumit Pal, Tathagata Dasgupta, Varadharajan Pundi Sridhar, Wayne Mather, and Yilun Zhang.

To our families (Oskar's Johanna, Stella, Molly; Tomaz's Anica, Blaz, Brina) and friends: Thank you for putting up with the late nights and endless shop talk. Your encouragement kept us going. Finally, a shoutout goes to the broader graph and GenAI community—your innovations and discussions pushed us to write something practical and useful. This book is as much a product of your collective energy as it is ours.

about this book

Essential GraphRAG was written to guide readers in enhancing retrieval-augmented generation (RAG) systems by integrating knowledge graphs with large language models (LLMs). The book aims to address the limitations of LLMs, such as outdated knowledge, hallucinations, and a lack of domain-specific data, by combining structured and unstructured data through practical methodologies and hands-on examples.

The primary goal of *Essential GraphRAG* is to demonstrate how knowledge graphs can improve the accuracy, performance, and traceability of RAG systems in generative AI applications. The book explores grounding LLMs with both structured and unstructured data, offering a comprehensive guide to building a GraphRAG system from scratch. It combines years of expertise in graphs, machine learning, and application development to present stable architectural patterns in a rapidly evolving field. Readers will learn to implement GraphRAG without relying on existing frameworks, extract structured knowledge from text, and develop applications that blend vector-based and graph-based retrieval methods, including Microsoft's GraphRAG approach. The book encourages active participation through its liveBook discussion forum to refine content and deepen collective understanding.

Who should read this book

This book is intended for data scientists, software engineers, and developers seeking to enhance their generative AI toolkit by incorporating knowledge graphs into RAG workflows. It is ideal for individuals with a basic understanding of Python, LLMs, and data processing concepts who are eager to address LLM limitations, like factual inaccuracies or knowledge cutoffs. The structured approach caters to a broad audience: junior practitioners will gain a solid foundation in GraphRAG techniques, while experienced professionals will find advanced strategies, like Microsoft's GraphRAG implementation, and fresh perspectives to elevate their work. Domain experts in fields like legal, literature, or business intelligence, where structured data and narrative summarization are critical, will also benefit from the practical examples and methodologies.

How this book is organized: A road map

The book is organized into eight chapters, some building on the previous to guide readers from foundational concepts to advanced GraphRAG implementations:

- Chapter 1 introduces LLMs, their limitations (e.g., knowledge cutoff, hallucinations), and how RAG with knowledge graphs can overcome these issues using structured and unstructured data.
- Chapter 2 covers embeddings, vector similarity search, and hybrid search techniques, providing a practical walkthrough of a RAG application, starting with unstructured data.
- Chapter 3 delves into sophisticated retrieval methods to enhance RAG performance.
- Chapter 4 teaches you how to convert natural language questions into Cypher queries for graph databases, enhancing retrieval flexibility.
- Chapter 5 explores autonomous RAG systems that use LLMs and graphs for complex tasks.
- Chapter 6 guides readers through extracting structured data from text (e.g., legal contracts) and building knowledge graphs, using tools like Neo4j.
- Chapter 7 explores Microsoft's GraphRAG pipeline using *The Odyssey*, focusing on entity/relationship extraction, community detection, and global/local search retrieval for summarization-heavy RAG applications.
- Chapter 8 focuses on assessing the performance and reliability of GraphRAG systems.

The book progresses from understanding LLM constraints and basic RAG to advanced graph-enhanced techniques, including Microsoft's innovative summarization-focused approach, culminating in practical applications and evaluation

About the code

This book contains many examples of source code both in numbered listings and in line with normal text. In both cases, source code is formatted in a `fixed-width font like this` to separate it from ordinary text.

In many cases, the original source code has been reformatted; we've added line breaks and reworked indentation to accommodate the available page space in the book. In some cases, even this was not enough, and listings include line-continuation markers (➥). Additionally, comments in the source code have often been removed from the listings when the code is described in the text. Code annotations accompany many of the listings, highlighting important concepts.

Source code examples are available in the book's accompanying GitHub repository, https://github.com/tomasonjo/kg-rag. The repository contains Jupyter notebooks and Python scripts for each chapter, allowing readers to follow along with the book's content. The code is organized by chapter, making it easy to find specific examples and implementations. Additionally, the repository includes instructions for setting up the necessary environment and dependencies to run the code locally.

You can get executable snippets of code from the liveBook (online) version of this book at https://livebook.manning.com/book/essential-graphrag. The complete code for the examples in the book is also available for download from the Manning website at https://www.manning.com/books/essential-graphrag.

liveBook discussion forum

Purchase of *Essential GraphRAG* includes free access to liveBook, Manning's online reading platform. Using liveBook's exclusive discussion features, you can attach comments to the book globally or to specific sections or paragraphs. It's a snap to make notes for yourself, ask and answer technical questions, and receive help from the authors and other users. To access the forum, go to https://livebook.manning.com/book/essential-graphrag/discussion.

Manning's commitment to our readers is to provide a venue where a meaningful dialogue between individual readers and between readers and the authors can take place. It is not a commitment to any specific amount of participation on the part of the authors, whose contribution to the forum remains voluntary (and unpaid). We suggest you try asking them some challenging questions lest their interest stray! The forum and the archives of previous discussions will be accessible from the publisher's website as long as the book is in print.

about the authors

TOMAŽ BRATANIČ has extensive experience with graphs, machine learning, and generative AI. He has written an in-depth book about using graph algorithms in practical examples. Nowadays, he focuses on generative AI and LLMs by contributing to popular frameworks like LangChain and LlamaIndex and writing blog posts about LLM-based applications.

OSKAR HANE is a senior staff software engineer at Neo4j. He has over 20 years of experience as a software engineer and 10 years of experience working with Neo4j and knowledge graphs. He is currently leading the generative AI engineering team within Neo4j, with a focus on providing the best possible experience for other developers to build GenAI applications with Neo4j.

about the cover illustration

The figure on the cover of *Essential GraphRAG* is "Likanienne," or "A woman from Lika," taken from Balthasar Hacquet's *Illustrations de L'Illyrie et la Dalmatie.*

In those days, it was easy to identify where people lived and what their trade or station in life was just by their dress. Manning celebrates the inventiveness and initiative of the computer business with book covers based on the rich diversity of regional culture centuries ago, brought back to life by pictures from collections such as this one.

1 Improving LLM accuracy

This chapter covers

- Large language models
- Limitations of large language models
- Shortcomings of continuously finetuning a model
- Retrieval-augmented generation
- Combining structured and unstructured data to support all types of questions

Large language models (LLMs) have shown impressive abilities across a variety of domains, but they have significant limitations that affect their utility, particularly when tasked with generating accurate and up-to-date information. One widely adopted approach to addressing these limitations is retrieval-augmented generation (RAG), a workflow that combines an LLM with an external knowledge base to deliver accurate and current responses. By pulling data from trusted sources at run time, RAG can significantly reduce, though not completely eliminate, hallucinations, one of the most persistent challenges with LLMs. In addition, RAG allows systems to seamlessly bridge general knowledge with niche, domain-specific information that may not be well represented in the pretraining data of the model. Despite these advantages, RAG implementations have often focused solely on unstructured data, overlooking the potential of structured sources like knowledge graphs.

Knowledge graphs are structured representations of entities, their attributes, and their relationships, offering a semantic framework that bridges structured and unstructured data. For instance, a customer support transcript is unstructured text, while a product catalog or user database is structured. Bridging them means enabling a system to connect conversational mentions of "my recent laptop order" to the structured record of the exact model, purchase date, and warranty status. Knowledge graphs serve as a critical component to RAG by enabling accurate, context-rich, and interconnected information retrieval—such as linking a customer query about a drug interaction to structured medical guidelines, prior case studies, and the patient's history in real time. Integrating knowledge graphs into RAG pipelines can overcome LLM limitations, enhance data retrieval, and facilitate a holistic approach to managing and using diverse data types across domains like healthcare, finance, and technical support.

This book is for developers, researchers, and data practitioners who want to build more robust, explainable, and capable RAG systems. You'll learn both how to augment existing RAG architectures with knowledge graphs and how to build new GraphRAG pipelines from scratch. Along the way, you'll gain practical skills in data modeling, graph construction, retrieval workflows, and system evaluation.

By the end of this book, you'll have a clear understanding of how LLMs, RAG, and knowledge graphs intersect to create robust systems capable of addressing complex queries and delivering accurate, reliable, and explainable results.

1.1 Introduction to LLMs

By now, you've likely encountered or heard about ChatGPT, one of the most prominent examples of conversational AI. ChatGPT is a conversational user interface developed by OpenAI and powered by LLMs, such as GPT-4 (OpenAI et al., 2024). LLMs are built on transformer architecture (Vaswani et al., 2017), which enables them to process and generate text efficiently. These models are trained on vast amounts of textual data, allowing them to learn patterns, grammar, context, and even some degree of reasoning. The training process involves feeding the model large datasets that include a diverse range of text with the primary objective of enabling the model to accurately predict the next word in a sequence. This extensive exposure enables the models to understand and generate human-like text based on the patterns they have learned from the data. For example, if you use "Never gonna" as input to an LLM, you might get a response similar to that shown in figure 1.1.

Figure 1.1 shows an LLM processing the input "Never gonna" and generating the output "give you up." This highlights how an LLM relies on patterns and associations it learned during training, such as those derived from common cultural references, including popular music. The quality and relevance of these responses depend significantly on the diversity and depth of the training dataset, which determines the LLM's ability to recognize and replicate such patterns.

Figure 1.1 LLMs are trained to predict the next word.

While LLMs excel at generating contextually appropriate text, they are far more than just autocomplete systems. Their remarkable ability to follow instructions and adapt to a wide range of tasks is impressive. For example, as shown in figure 1.2, you can ask ChatGPT to generate a haiku about a specific topic in a particular style. This capability illustrates not just pattern recognition but an understanding of task-specific instructions, enabling creative and nuanced outputs well beyond simple text prediction.

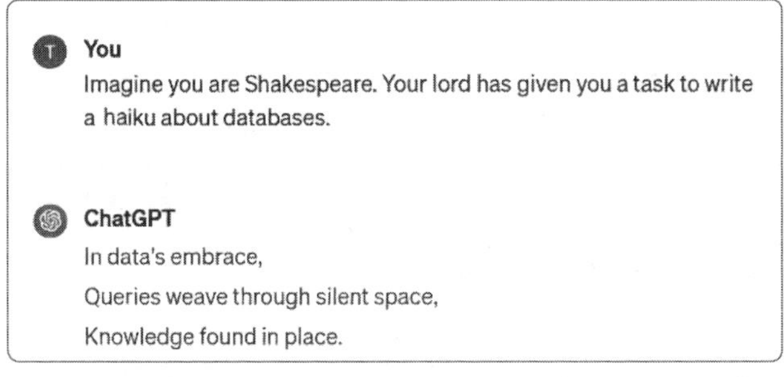

Figure 1.2 Writing a haiku with ChatGPT

The ability of LLMs to follow instructions and generate diverse, complex outputs, whether crafting a haiku or providing structured responses, goes beyond simply predicting the next word in a sequence. This ability to understand and execute detailed instructions makes LLMs uniquely suited for a wide variety of tasks. In this book, you will use this instruction-following ability to design and refine RAG pipelines. By tapping into instruction-following capabilities, you can integrate retrieval components more effectively, tailor responses to specific contexts, and optimize your systems for accuracy and usability.

ChatGPT's breadth of general knowledge is equally remarkable. For example, figure 1.3 illustrates ChatGPT's response when prompted about the first manned moon landing.

If you verify this response with external information from NASA or Wikipedia, you can observe that the model produces an accurate response with no false information. Such a response might give you the impression that an LLM constructs a vast database of facts from which it can retrieve when prompted. However, the model doesn't store specific facts, events, or information from its training dataset. Instead, it develops

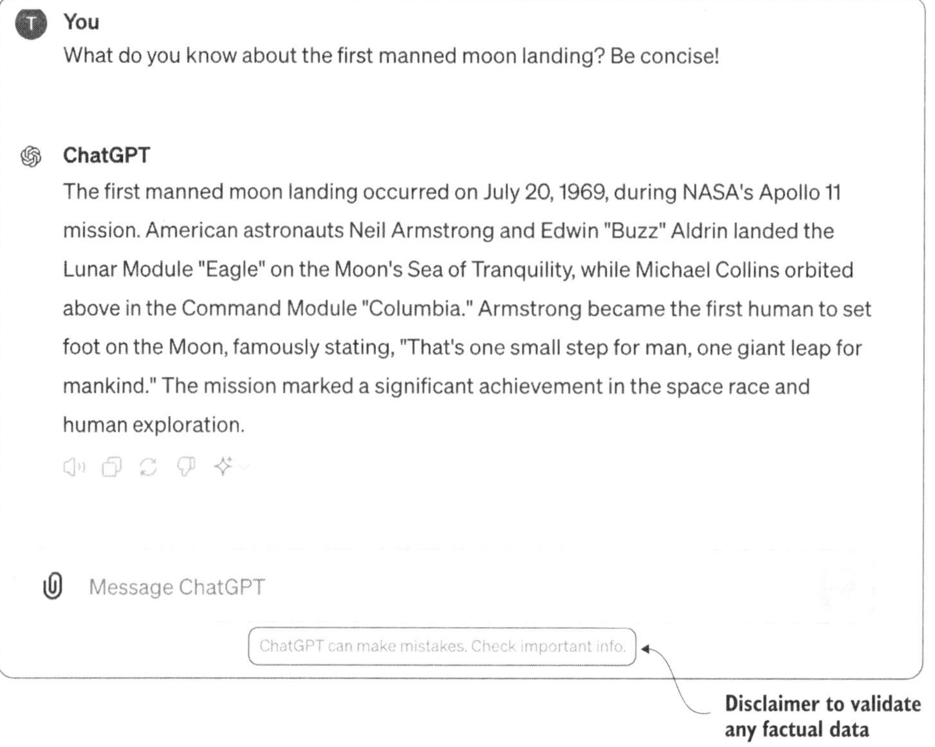

Figure 1.3 Retrieving factual information from ChatGPT

complex mathematical representations of the language it is trained on. Remember, the LLMs are based on the transformer, which is a deep learning architecture based on neural networks to predict the next word, as shown in figure 1.4.

Figure 1.4 illustrates a neural network predicting the next word in a sequence, similar to how LLMs function. The central part shows the network with multiple layers of neurons, connected by lines that represent the flow of information. Each connection has a weight, such as the example value 0.04, which influences the strength of the connection. During training, the model learns the values of these weights to improve its predictions. When asked about a specific historical event, an LLM doesn't recall the event from its training data. Instead, it generates a response based on the learned weights in its neural network, similar to predicting the next word in a sequence. Therefore, while LLMs can provide seemingly knowledgeable answers, their responses are based on these learned weights rather than explicit memory. To quote Andrej Karpathy: "We kind of understand that they (LLMs) build and maintain some kind of a knowledge database, but even this knowledge base is very strange and imperfect and weird"(https://www.youtube.com/watch?v=zjkBMFhNj_g at 12:40).

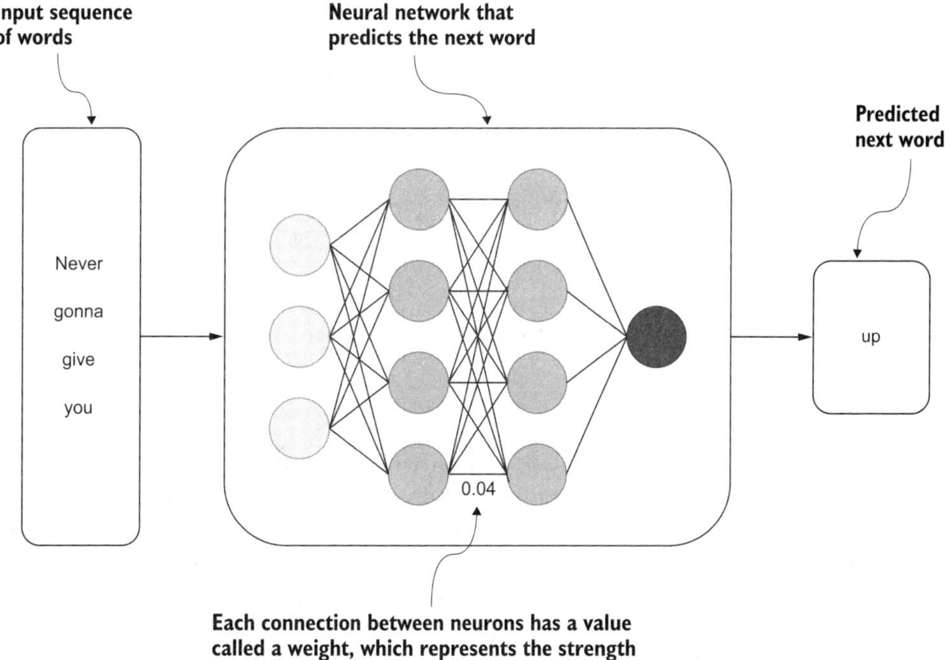

Figure 1.4 Neural network trained to predict the next word based on the input sequence of words

1.2 Limitations of LLMs

LLMs represent a groundbreaking step in the evolution of AI, offering remarkable capabilities across a range of applications. Yet, as with any transformative technology, they are not without their challenges and constraints. In the following section, we will delve into some of these limitations and their implications.

1.2.1 Knowledge cutoff problem

The most obvious limitation is that LLMs are unaware of events or information not included in their training dataset. At this moment, ChatGPT is aware of information that occurred up to October 2023. For example, if you asked ChatGPT about an event in 2024, you would get a response similar to that shown in figure 1.5.

In the context of LLMs, the *knowledge cutoff date* refers to the most recent point at which the model's training data includes information. The model has access to a broad spectrum of text data containing information about events up to this date from diverse sources, which it utilizes to generate responses and provide information. Anything that has occurred or been published after this cutoff date is unknown to the model as it was not included in the training dataset; therefore, it cannot provide information about events, developments, or research that occurred after the cutoff date.

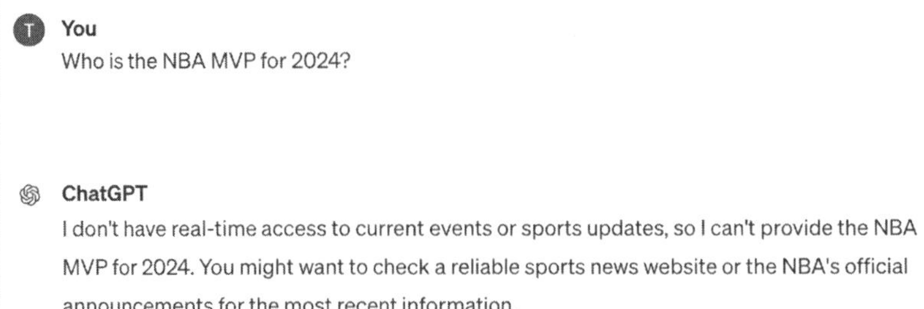

Figure 1.5 Example of a knowledge cutoff date disclaimer

1.2.2 Outdated information

A less obvious limitation is that LLMs can sometimes provide outdated responses. While they can deliver detailed and accurate information up until their knowledge cutoff, they may not reflect recent developments. For instance, as of late 2023, Mark Cuban sold his majority stake in the Dallas Mavericks franchise to the Adelson family and the Dumonts while retaining a minority share. This major update highlights how information that was correct in the past can become outdated. For example, in a query about the Dallas Mavericks, a response shown in figure 1.6 reflects Cuban as the sole owner, which is no longer accurate (Rader, 2023).

Figure 1.6 Sometimes ChatGPT responds with outdated information.

This highlights the importance of regularly updating training data for models or enabling them to access real-time information. With continuously evolving events and facts, even small details like ownership structures can significantly impact how we perceive an organization or individual. This limitation underlines the importance of ensuring AI systems remain accurate and relevant in dynamic environments.

1.2.3 Pure hallucinations

Another well-known limitation of LLMs is their tendency to provide assertive, confident answers—even when those answers contain incorrect or fabricated information.

One might assume that, despite their knowledge cutoff dates, these models provide accurate factual data up to that point. However, even information about events that occurred before the cutoff can be unreliable.

A striking example of this occurred when lawyers in the United States submitted bogus, fictitious legal citations to a court, unaware that they had been generated by ChatGPT (Neumeister, 2023). These kinds of confident inaccuracies are commonly known as hallucinations, where the model outputs information that sounds plausible but is factually incorrect or entirely fabricated. External references such as URLs, academic citations, or identifiers like WikiData IDs are especially prone to this behavior.

Hallucinations occur because LLMs are not reasoning engines. They are probabilistic language models trained to predict what sounds like a good next token, based on patterns in their training data. They don't know facts the way humans do. Rather, they generate text by guessing the most likely continuation, regardless of whether it's true. This fundamental difference between statistical pattern matching and actual understanding is what separates LLMs from human cognition.

To illustrate this, we can ask ChatGPT to provide the WikiData ID of the Dallas Mavericks NBA franchise. As shown in figure 1.7, the model confidently returns an identifier—but it's incorrect.

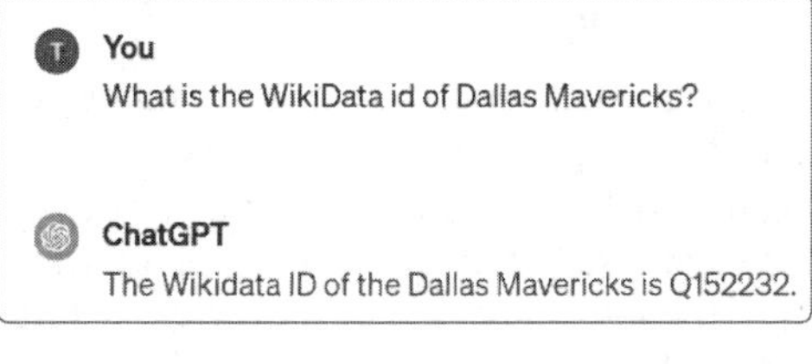

Figure 1.7 ChatGPT can produce responses with incorrect information.

The model assertively replied with an ID that follows the WikiData format. However, if you verify this information, you can observe that Q152232 is the WikiData ID of the movie titled *Womanlight* (https://www.wikidata.org/wiki/Q152232). Therefore, users must recognize that LLMs, while often informative, are not infallible and can produce erroneous information. It's crucial to approach their responses critically and verify their accuracy through reliable external sources, especially in contexts where precision and factual correctness are central.

1.2.4 Lack of private information

If you were building a company chatbot using an LLM, you'd likely want it to answer questions involving internal or proprietary information that isn't publicly available. In such cases, even if the information or events occurred before the LLM's knowledge cutoff date, they wouldn't have been part of its training data. As a result, the model cannot generate accurate responses for such queries, as illustrated in figure 1.8.

You
What is customer churn rate of ChatGPT users?

ChatGPT
The customer churn rate for ChatGPT users is not publicly disclosed by OpenAI. Customer churn rate typically refers to the percentage of customers who stop using a service during a certain time frame. Since OpenAI does not publicly release specific user data or statistics like churn rates, this information is not available.

Figure 1.8 ChatGPT didn't have access to some private or confidential information during training.

One potential solution would be to make the company's internal information publicly available in the hope that it gets included in the training dataset of an LLM. However, this approach is neither practical nor secure. Instead, we will explore and demonstrate more effective strategies to overcome these limitations while maintaining data privacy and control.

Note on other limitations of LLMs

While this book will focus on the limitations of LLMs in providing factually correct and up-to-date information in responses, it's important to acknowledge that LLMs also have other restrictions. Some of these include

- *Bias in responses*—LLMs can sometimes generate biased responses, reflecting biases present in the training data.
- *Lack of understanding and context*—LLMs, despite their complexity, do not truly understand the text. They process language based on patterns learned from data, which means they can miss nuances and contextual subtleties.
- *Vulnerability to prompt injection*—LLMs are susceptible to prompt injection attacks, where malicious users craft inputs to manipulate the model into generating inappropriate, biased, or harmful responses. This vulnerability poses significant challenges for ensuring the security and integrity of LLM applications in real-world scenarios.
- *Inconsistent responses*—LLMs can produce different answers to the same question across multiple interactions. This inconsistency arises from their probabilistic nature and lack of persistent memory, which can hinder their usefulness in applications that require stability and repeatability.

This book is dedicated to exploring and addressing the specific limitations of LLMs concerning the generation of factually accurate and up-to-date responses. Although we recognize other limitations of LLMs, our discussion will not cover them.

1.3 Overcoming the limitations of LLMs

LLMs are powerful tools, but they often face limitations when handling domain-specific questions or accessing specialized, up-to-date knowledge. Implementing a ChatGPT-like application in a business environment requires outputs that are both precise and factually accurate. To overcome these challenges, we can inject domain-specific knowledge into LLMs using approaches like supervised finetuning and RAG. In this section, we'll explore how these methods work and how they can be applied to inject domain-specific knowledge into LLMs.

1.3.1 Supervised finetuning

At first, many of us thought we would overcome the limitations of LLMs with additional training. For example, we could overcome the knowledge cutoff date limitation by continuously updating the model. However, to address this limitation effectively, we first need to better understand the training of an LLM. The training of an LLM like ChatGPT can be split into the following four stages, as described by Andrew Karpathy (https://www.youtube.com/watch?v=bZQun8Y4L2A):

1. *Pretraining*—The model reads a vast amount of text, often more than a trillion tokens, to learn basic language patterns. It practices predicting what word comes next in a sentence. This is the foundational step, like learning vocabulary and grammar before you can write. This is the most resource-intensive phase, which can require thousands of GPUs and can take months of continuous training.
2. *Supervised finetuning*—The model is given specific examples of high-quality conversations to improve its ability to respond like a helpful assistant. It continues to practice language but now with a focus on generating useful and accurate responses. Think of it as moving from basic language learning to practicing conversation skills. This requires significantly fewer resources than pretraining and can nowadays even run on a single laptop for smaller LLMs.
3. *Reward modeling*—The model learns to distinguish between good and bad responses by comparing different answers to the same questions. It's like having a coach who shows the model what a good performance looks like so it can aim to replicate that quality.
4. *Reinforcement learning*—The model interacts with users or simulated environments to further refine its responses based on feedback. It's similar to learning a sport: practicing not just by drills but by playing actual games and learning from the experience.

Since the pretraining phase is costly and time consuming and, therefore, not feasible for continuous updating, the idea was to use the supervised finetuning phase to overcome the limitations of LLMs. During the supervised finetuning phase, you supply the language model with specific examples of input prompts along with the corresponding desired outputs you aim for the model to produce. One such example is shown in figure 1.9.

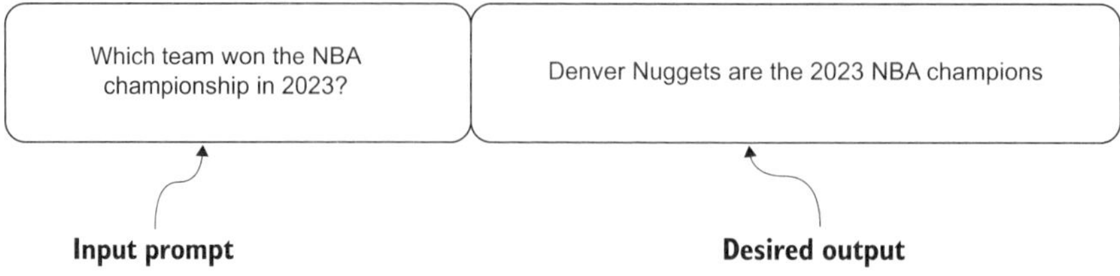

Figure 1.9 Sample record of a supervised finetuning dataset

Figure 1.9 shows an example of a question–answer pair that could be used to finetune an LLM. In this example, the input prompt or the question is about which team won the 2023 NBA championship, and the corresponding answer is the Denver Nuggets. The theory was that, through this example, the LLM would include this fact in its mathematical representation of the language and be able to answer questions revolving around the 2023 NBA champions. Some research studies have shown that supervised finetuning can improve LLM factuality (Tian et al., 2023). However, other studies using different methods also show that LLMs struggle to learn new factual information through finetuning (Ovadia et al., 2023).

While supervised finetuning can enhance the overall knowledge of a model, it remains a complex and evolving field of research. As such, deploying a reliable, finetuned language model in a production environment poses significant challenges at the current stage of technological development. Fortunately, a more efficient and simpler method to address the knowledge limitations of LLMs exists.

1.3.2 *Retrieval-augmented generation*

The second strategy for improving LLM accuracy and overcoming its limitations is the RAG workflow, which combines an LLM with an external knowledge base to deliver accurate and up-to-date responses. Instead of depending on an LLM's internal knowledge, relevant facts or information are provided directly in the input prompt (Lewis et al., 2020). This concept (RAG) uses the LLM's strengths in understanding and generating natural language, while factual information is supplied in the prompt, reducing dependence on the LLM's internal knowledge base and consequently hallucinations.

The RAG workflow operates in two main stages:

- Retrieval
- Augmented generation

In the retrieval stage, relevant information is located from an external knowledge base or database. During the augmented generation stage, this retrieved information is combined with the user's input to enhance the context provided to the LLM, enabling it to generate a response grounded in reliable, external facts. The RAG workflow is illustrated in figure 1.10.

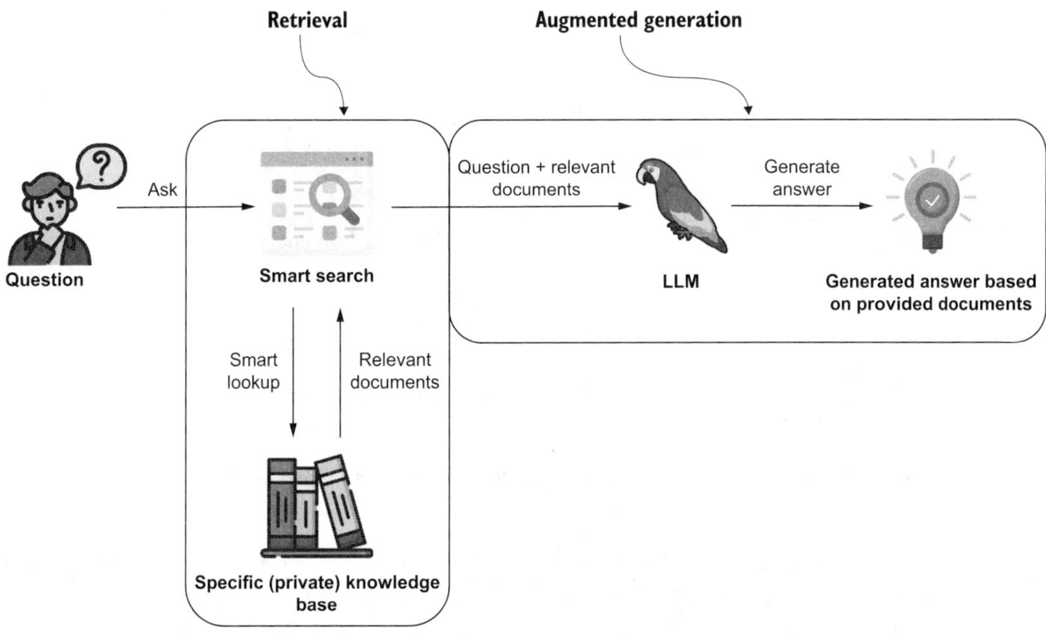

Figure 1.10 Providing relevant information to the LLM as part of the input

As mentioned, LLMs are great at understanding natural language and following instructions in the prompt. In the RAG workflow, the goal shifts to task-oriented response generation, where LLMs follow a set of instructions. The process involves utilizing a retrieval tool to fetch relevant documents from a specific knowledge base. The LLM then generates answers based on the provided documents, ensuring responses are accurate, contextually relevant, and aligned with specific guidelines. This systematic approach transforms the answer generation process into a targeted task of inspecting and using the retrieved information to produce the final answer. An example of providing factual information in the input prompt is shown in figure 1.11.

Figure 1.11 illustrates an example of how an LLM processes follows the prompt instructions of a RAG workflow. The prompt highlights the importance of using retrieved context to ensure accurate and relevant responses and can be broken down into

- *Provided context*—A factual statement that introduces relevant information—in this case, identifying the Denver Nuggets as the 2023 NBA champions with a 4:1 victory over the Miami Heat. This acts as the knowledge base input for the LLM.
- *User query*—A specific question, "Who won the 2023 NBA championship?" which directs the LLM to extract relevant information from the provided context.
- *Generated answer*—The LLM's response is aligned with the retrieved context: "The Denver Nuggets won the 2023 NBA championship."

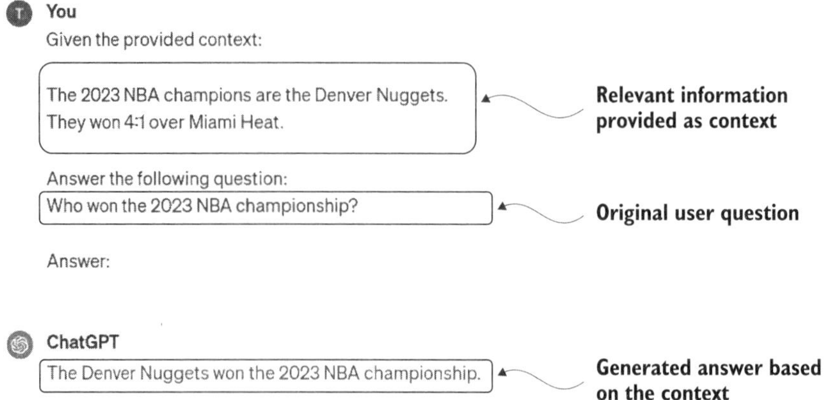

Figure 1.11 Providing relevant information to the answer as part of the prompt

You might wonder what the advantage of the RAG process is if the user has to provide both the context and the questions. In practice, the retrieval system operates independently from the user. The user only needs to provide the question, while the retrieval process occurs behind the scenes, as illustrated in figure 1.12.

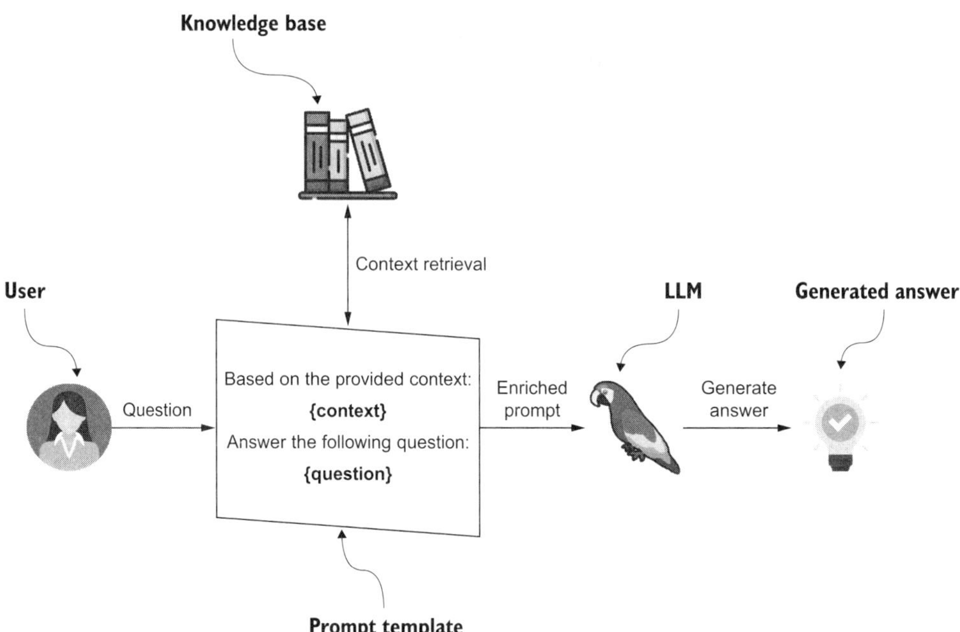

Figure 1.12 Populating the relevant data from the user and knowledge base into the prompt template and then passing it to an LLM to generate the final answer

In the RAG process, the user starts by asking a question. Behind the scenes, the system turns that question into a search query and retrieves relevant information from sources like company documents, knowledge articles, or databases. Advanced retrieval algorithms find the most suitable content, which is then combined with the original question to form an enriched prompt. This prompt is sent to an LLM, which generates a response based on both the question and the retrieved context. The entire retrieval process is automatic, and no extra input is required beyond the original question from the user. This makes RAG both seamless and effective, improving factual accuracy while reducing the chance of hallucinated answers.

The RAG approach has gained mainstream popularity due to its simplicity and efficiency. It is now also part of the ChatGPT interface, where the LLM can use Web Search to search for relevant information before generating the final answer. Users of the paid version of ChatGPT may be familiar with the RAG process as depicted in figure 1.13.

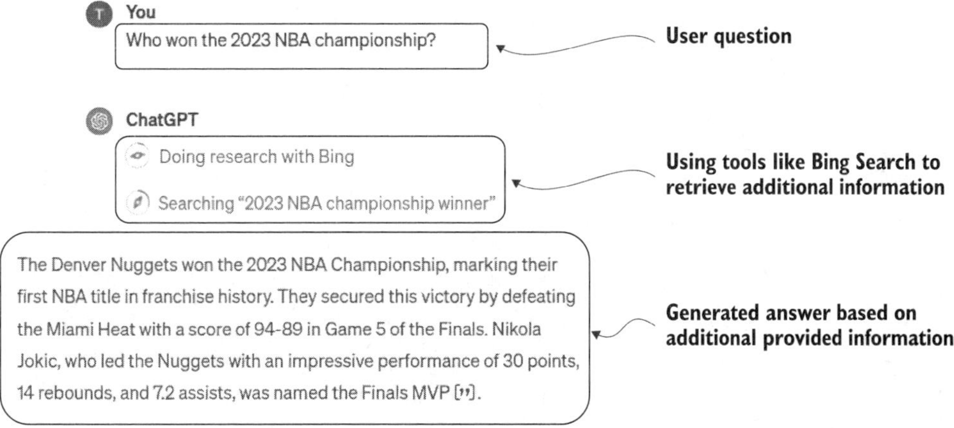

Figure 1.13 ChatGPT uses Web Search to find relevant information to generate an up-to-date answer.

While the exact implementation of RAG in ChatGPT is not publicly disclosed, we can try to infer what it does under the hood. When the LLM decides, for whatever reason, that it needs to pull additional information, it can input a query into Web Search. We don't know precisely how it navigates through search results, parses information from web pages, or decides that it has retrieved sufficient information. Nevertheless, we know that it used `2023 NBA championship winner` keyword as input to Web Search and generated the final response based on the information available on the official NBA website (https://www.nba.com/playoffs/2023/the-finals).

1.4 Knowledge graphs as the data storage for RAG applications

When planning to implement a RAG application, choosing the right storage solution is important. While there are many database options, we argue that knowledge graphs and graph databases are especially well suited for most RAG applications. A knowledge graph is a data structure that uses nodes to represent concepts and entities and relationships to connect these nodes. An example knowledge graph is shown in figure 1.14.

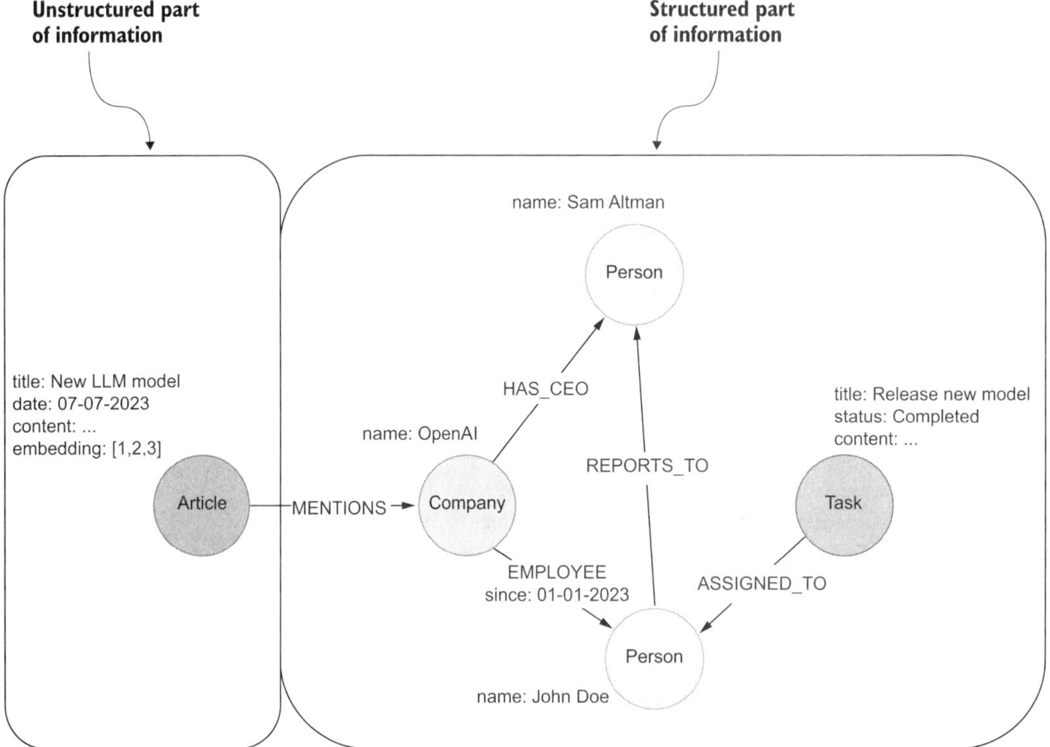

Figure 1.14 A knowledge graph can store complex structured and unstructured data in a single database system.

Knowledge graphs are highly versatile, capable of storing both structured information (such as employee details, task statuses, and company hierarchies) and unstructured information (such as article contents). This dual capability, as illustrated in figure 1.14, makes them uniquely suited for complex RAG applications. Structured data allows for precise and efficient querying to answer questions such as, "How many tasks are assigned to a specific employee?" or "Which employees report to a particular manager?" For example, in figure 1.14, structured data such as "Sam Altman is the CEO of

OpenAI" or "John Doe has been an employee of OpenAI since 01-01-2023" can be directly queried to answer questions like "Who is the CEO of OpenAI?" or "How long has John Doe been with the company?" Similarly, structured relationships like "John Doe is assigned to a task with the status Completed" enable precise queries such as "Which tasks have been completed by employees?" or "Who is assigned to specific tasks at OpenAI?" This capability is critical for generating actionable insights from complex, interconnected data.

On the other hand, unstructured data, such as article text, complements structured data by providing rich contextual information that adds depth and nuance. For instance, the unstructured article node in figure 1.14 provides details about a new LLM model and embeddings, but without a structured framework, it cannot answer specific queries like "How is this article related to OpenAI employees?"

Importantly, unstructured data alone cannot answer all types of questions. While it can provide insights for open-ended or fuzzy queries, it lacks the structure needed for precise operations such as filtering, counting, or aggregating. For example, answering "How many tasks are completed within a company?" or "Which employees are assigned to tasks related to OpenAI?" requires structured relationships and attributes, as depicted in the right-hand side of figure 1.14. Without structured data, these types of queries would require exhaustive text parsing and inference, which are computationally expensive and often imprecise. By integrating structured and unstructured information in the same framework, knowledge graphs enable the seamless blending of both worlds, making them a powerful tool for answering a broad range of questions efficiently and accurately in RAG applications. Moreover, explicit connections between unstructured and structured data unlock advanced retrieval strategies such as linking entities in text to graph nodes or contextualizing structured results with source passages that would be difficult or impossible to achieve using either type of data alone.

Summary

- LLMs, such as ChatGPT, are built on transformer architecture, enabling them to process and generate text efficiently by learning patterns from extensive textual data.
- While LLMs exhibit remarkable abilities in natural language understanding and generation, they have inherent limitations, such as a knowledge cutoff, the potential to generate outdated or hallucinated information, and an inability to access private or domain-specific knowledge.
- Continuous finetuning of LLMs to enhance their internal knowledge base is not practical due to resource constraints and the complexity of updating the models regularly.
- RAG addresses LLM limitations by combining them with external knowledge bases, providing accurate, context-rich responses by injecting relevant facts directly into the input prompt.

- RAG implementations have traditionally focused on unstructured data sources, limiting their scope and effectiveness for tasks requiring structured, precise, and interconnected information.
- Knowledge graphs use nodes and relationships to represent and connect entities and concepts, integrating structured and unstructured data to provide a holistic data representation.
- Integrating knowledge graphs into RAG workflows enhances their capability to retrieve and organize contextually relevant data, allowing LLMs to generate accurate, reliable, and explainable responses.

2 Vector similarity search and hybrid search

This chapter covers

- Introduction to embeddings, embedding models, vector space, and vector similarity search
- How vector similarity fits in RAG applications
- A practical walkthrough of a RAG application using vector similarity search
- Adding full-text search to the RAG application to see how enabling a hybrid search approach can improve results

Creating a knowledge graph can be an iterative process where you start with unstructured data and then add structure to it. This is often the case when you have a lot of unstructured data and you want to start using it to answer questions.

This chapter will look at how we can use RAG to answer questions using unstructured data. We'll look at how to use vector similarity search and hybrid search to find relevant information and how to use that information to generate an answer. In later chapters, we'll look at what techniques we can use to improve the retriever and generator to get better results when there's some structure to the data.

In data science and machine learning, embedding models and vector similarity search are important tools for handling complex data. This chapter looks at how these technologies turn complicated data, like text and images, into uniform formats called embeddings.

In this chapter, we will cover the basics of embedding models and vector similarity search, explaining why they are useful, how they are used, and the challenges they help solve in RAG applications. To follow along, you'll need access to a running, blank Neo4j instance. This can be a local installation or a cloud-hosted instance; just make sure it's empty. You can follow the implementation directly in the accompanying Jupyter notebook available here: https://github.com/tomasonjo/kg-rag/blob/main/notebooks/ch02.ipynb.

2.1 Components of a RAG architecture

In a RAG application, there are two main components: a *retriever* and a *generator*. The retriever finds relevant information, and the generator uses that information to create a response. Vector similarity search is used in the retriever to find relevant information; this is explained in more detail later. Let's dig into both these components.

2.1.1 The retriever

The retriever is the first component of a RAG application. Its purpose is to find relevant information and pass that information to the generator. How the retriever finds the relevant information is not implied in the RAG framework, but the most common way is to use vector similarity search. Let's look at what's needed to prepare data for the retriever to be successful using vector similarity search.

VECTOR INDEX

While a vector index isn't strictly required for vector similarity search, it's highly recommended. A vector index is a data structure (like a map) that stores vectors in a way that makes it easy to search for similar vectors. When using a vector index, the retriever method is often referred to as an *approximate nearest neighbor search*. This is because the vector index doesn't find the exact nearest neighbors, but it finds vectors that are very close to the nearest neighbor. This is a tradeoff between speed and accuracy. The vector index is much faster than a brute-force search, but it's not as accurate.

VECTOR SIMILARITY SEARCH FUNCTION

A *vector similarity search* function is a function that takes a vector as input and returns a list of similar vectors. This function might use a vector index to find similar vectors, or it might use some other (brute-force) method. The important thing is that it returns a list of similar vectors.

The two most common vector similarity search functions are cosine similarity and Euclidean distance. *Euclidean distance* represents the content and intensity of the text, which is not as important in most cases covered in this book. *Cosine similarity* is a measure of the angle between two vectors. In our text-embedding case, this angle represents how similar two texts are in their meaning. The cosine similarity function takes two vectors as input and returns a number between 0 and 1; 0 means the vectors are completely different, and 1 means they are identical. Cosine similarity is considered the best fit for text chatbots, and it's the one we'll use in this book.

EMBEDDING MODEL

The result from a semantic classification of text is called an *embedding*. Any text you want to match using vector similarity search must be converted into an embedding. This is done using an embedding model, and it's important that the embedding model stays the same throughout the RAG application. If you want to change the embedding model, you must repopulate the vector index.

Embeddings are lists of numbers, and the length of the list is called the embedding dimension. The embedding dimension is important because it determines how much information the embedding can hold. The higher the embedding dimension, the more computationally expensive it is to work with the embedding, both when generating the embedding as well as when performing vector similarity search.

An *embedding* is a way to represent complex data as a set of numbers in a simpler, lower-dimensional space. Think of it as translating data into a format that a computer can easily understand and work with.

Embedding models provide a uniform way to represent different types of data. Input to an embedding model can be any complex data, and the output is a vector. For instance, in dealing with text, an embedding model will take words or sentences and turn them into vectors, which are lists of numbers. The model is trained to ensure that these number lists capture essential aspects of the original words, such as their meaning or context.

TEXT CHUNKING

Text chunking is the process of splitting up text into smaller pieces. This is done to improve the accuracy of the retriever. The presence of smaller pieces of text means that the embedding is narrower and more specific; thus the retriever will find more relevant information when searching.

Text chunking is very important and not easy to get right. You need to think about how to split up the text: Should it be sentences, paragraphs, semantic meaning, or something else? Should you use a sliding window, or should you use a fixed size? How big should the chunks be?

There are no right answers to these questions, and it depends on the use case, data, and domain. But it's important to think about these questions and try different approaches to find the best solution for your use case.

RETRIEVER PIPELINE

Once all pieces are in place, the retriever pipeline is quite simple. It takes a query as input, converts it into an embedding using the embedding model, and then uses the vector similarity search function to find similar embeddings. In the naive case, the retriever pipeline then just returns the source chunks, which then are passed to the generator. But in most cases, the retriever pipeline needs to do some postprocessing to find the best chunks to pass to the generator. We'll get to more advanced strategies in the next chapter.

2.1.2 The generator

The *generator* is the second component of a RAG application. It uses the information found by the retriever to generate a response. The generator is often an LLM, but one benefit of RAG over finetuning or relying on a model's base knowledge is that the models don't need to be as large. This is because the retriever finds relevant information, so the generator doesn't need to know everything. It does need to know how to use the information found by the retriever to create a response. This is a much smaller task than knowing everything.

So we're using the language model for its ability to generate text, not for its knowledge. This means we can use smaller language models, which are faster and cheaper to run. It also means that we can trust that the language model will base its response on the information found by the retriever and therefore make fewer things up and hallucinate less.

2.2 RAG using vector similarity search

There are a few pieces needed to implement a RAG application using vector similarity search. We'll go through each of them in this chapter. The goal is to show how to implement a RAG application using vector similarity search and how to use the information found by the retriever to generate a response. Figure 2.1 illustrates the data flow for the finished RAG application.

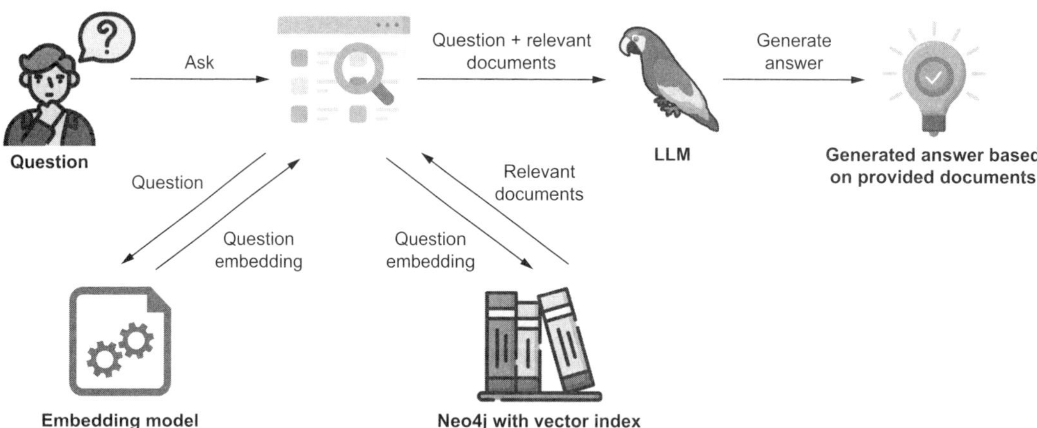

Figure 2.1 The data flow for this RAG application using vector similarity search

We need to separate the application into two stages:

- Data setup
- Query time

We'll start by looking at the data setup, and then we'll look at what the application will do at query time.

2.2.1 Application data setup

From earlier sections, we know that we need to process the data a bit to be able to place it in the embedding model vector space to perform vector similarity search at run time. The pieces needed are

- A text corpus
- Text-chunking function
- Embedding model
- Database with vector similarity search ability

We will go through these pieces one by one and show how they contribute to the application data setup.

The data will be stored in text chunks in a database, and the vector index will be populated with the embeddings of the text chunks. Later, at run time, when a user asks a question, the question will be embedded using the same embedding model as the text chunks, and then the vector index will be used to find similar text chunks. Figure 2.2 shows the data flow for the application data setup.

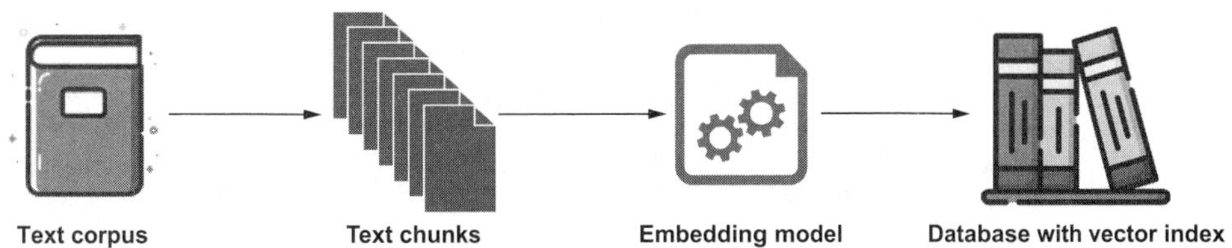

Figure 2.2 The pieces in the pipeline for the application data setup

2.2.2 The text corpus

The text we will be using in this example is a paper titled "Einstein's Patents and Inventions" (Caudhuri, 2017). Even though LLMs are well aware of Albert Einstein, we show that RAG works by asking very specific questions and comparing them with the answers we get from the paper versus answers we get from an LLM.

2.2.3 Text chunking

With an LLM having a large enough context window, we can use the whole paper as a single chunk. But to get better results, we'll split the paper into smaller chunks and use every few hundred characters as a chunk. The chunk size that yields the best results varies on a case-by-case basis, so make sure to experiment with different chunk sizes.

In this case, we also want to have some overlap between the chunks. This is because we want to be able to find answers that span multiple chunks. So we'll use a sliding window with a size of 500 characters and an overlap of 40 characters. This will make the index a bit bigger, but it will also make the retriever more accurate.

To help the embedding model better classify the semantics of each chunk, we will only chunk at spaces, so we don't have broken words at the start and end of each chunk. This function takes a text, chunk size (number of characters), overlap (number of characters), and an optional argument whether to split on any character or on whitespaces only and returns a list of chunks.

Listing 2.1 The text-chunking function

```
def chunk_text(text, chunk_size, overlap, split_on_whitespace_only=True):
    chunks = []
    index = 0

    while index < len(text):
        if split_on_whitespace_only:
            prev_whitespace = 0
            left_index = index - overlap
            while left_index >= 0:
                if text[left_index] == " ":
                    prev_whitespace = left_index
                    break
                left_index -= 1
            next_whitespace = text.find(" ", index + chunk_size)
            if next_whitespace == -1:
                next_whitespace = len(text)
            chunk = text[prev_whitespace:next_whitespace].strip()
            chunks.append(chunk)
            index = next_whitespace + 1
        else:
            start = max(0, index - overlap + 1)
            end = min(index + chunk_size + overlap, len(text))
            chunk = text[start:end].strip()
            chunks.append(chunk)
            index += chunk_size

    return chunks


chunks = chunk_text(text, 500, 40)


print(len(chunks)) # 89 chunks in total
```

Defines the function to chunk text

Calls the function and get chunks back

Prints the length of the chunks list. The majority of the function is just to make sure that we don't split individual words but only split on spaces.

2.2.4 Embedding model

When choosing an embedding model, it's important to think about what kind of data you want to match. In this case, we want to match text, so we'll use a text-embedding model. Throughout this book, we will use both embedding models and LLMs from OpenAI, but there are many alternatives out there. `all-MiniLM-L12-v2` via Sentence Transformers (https://mng.bz/nZZ2) from Hugging Face is a great alternative to OpenAI's embedding models, and it's very easy to use and can run on your local CPU.

Once we have decided on a embedding model, we need to make sure that we use the same model throughout the RAG application. This is because the vector index is populated with vectors from the embedding model, so if we change the embedding model, we need to repopulate the vector index. To embed the chunks using OpenAI's embedding models, we'll use the following code.

Listing 2.2 Embedding chunks

```
def embed(texts):                                                    # Defines the function to embed chunks
    response = open_ai_client.embeddings.create(
        input=texts,
        model="text-embedding-3-small",
    )
    return list(map(lambda n: n.embedding, response.data))

embeddings = embed(chunks)                                           # Calls the function and get embeddings back

print(len(embeddings)) # 89, matching the number of chunks           # Prints the length of the embeddings list
print(len(embeddings[0])) # 1536 dimensions                          # Prints the length of the first embedding
```

2.2.5 Database with vector similarity search function

Now that we have the embeddings, we need to store them so we can perform a similarity search later. In this book, we will use Neo4j as our database, since it has a built-in vector index and it's easy to use; later in the book we will use Neo4j for its graph capabilities.

The data model we'll use at this stage is quite simple. We'll have a single node type `Chunk` with two properties: `text` and `embedding`. The `text` property will hold the text of the chunk, and the `embedding` property will hold the embedding of the chunk.

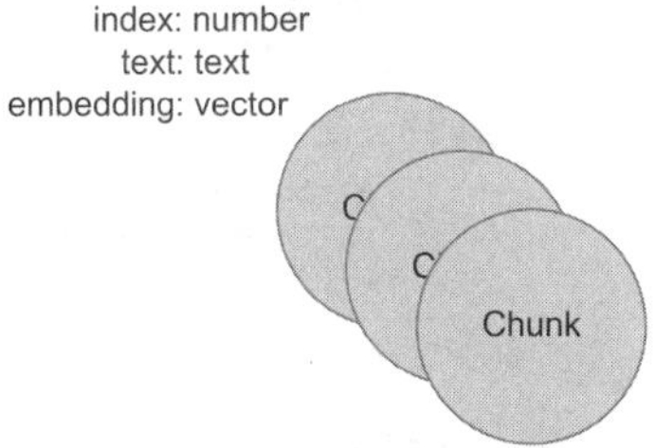

Figure 2.3 The data model

Figure 2.3 shows the simplistic data model that will be used to demonstrate how to implement a RAG application using vector similarity search.

First, let's create a vector index. One thing to keep in mind is that when we create the vector index, we need to define the number of dimensions the vectors will have. If you at any point in the future change the embedding model that outputs a different number of dimensions, you need to recreate the vector index.

As we saw in the code listing 2.2, the embedding model we used outputs vectors with 1,536 dimensions, so we'll use that as the number of dimensions when we create the vector index.

Listing 2.3 Creating a vector index in Neo4j

```
driver.execute_query("""CREATE VECTOR INDEX pdf IF NOT EXISTS
FOR (c:Chunk)
ON c.embedding""")
```

We will name the vector index `pdf` and it will be used to index nodes of type `Chunk` on the property `embedding` using the cosine similarity search function.

Now that we have a vector index, we can populate it with the embeddings. We will do this using Cypher, where we first create a node for each chunk and then set the `text` and `embedding` properties on the node using a Cypher loop. We're also storing an index on each `:Chunk` node, so we can easily find the chunk later.

Listing 2.4 Storing chunks and populating the vector index in Neo4j

```
cypher_query = '''
WITH $chunks as chunks, range(0, size($chunks)) AS index
UNWIND index AS i
WITH i, chunks[i] AS chunk, $embeddings[i] AS embedding
MERGE (c:Chunk {index: i})
SET c.text = chunk, c.embedding = embedding
'''

driver.execute_query(cypher_query, chunks=chunks, embeddings=embeddings)
```

To check what's in the database, we can run this Cypher query to get the `:Chunk` node with index 0.

Listing 2.5 Getting data from a chunk node in Neo4j

```
records, _, _ = driver.execute_query(
➥ "MATCH (c:Chunk) WHERE c.index = 0 RETURN c.embedding, c.text")

print(records[0]["c.text"][0:30])
print(records[0]["c.embedding"][0:3])
```

2.2.6 Performing vector search

Now that we have the vector index populated with the embeddings, we can perform a vector similarity search. First, we need to embed the question that we want to answer. We'll use the same embedding model as we used for the chunks, and we'll use the same function as we used to embed the chunks.

Listing 2.6 Embedding user question

```
question = "At what time was Einstein really interested
➥ in experimental works?"
question_embedding = embed([question])[0]
```

Now that we have the question embedded, we can perform a vector similarity search using Cypher.

Listing 2.7 Performing vector search in Neo4j

```
query = '''
CALL db.index.vector.queryNodes('pdf', 2, $question_embedding) YIELD node
➥ AS hits, score
RETURN hits.text AS text, score, hits.index AS index
'''
similar_records, _, _ = driver.execute_query(query,
     question_embedding=question_embedding)
```

The query returns the top two most similar chunks, and we can print the results to see what we got back. The code will print the following text chunks and their similarity scores.

Listing 2.8 Printing results

```
for record in similar_records:
    print(record["text"])
    print(record["score"], record["index"])
    print("======")
```

```
upbringing, his interest in inventions and patents was not unusual.
Being a manufacturer's son, Einstein grew upon in an environment of
➥ machines and instruments.
When his father's company obtained the contract to illuminate Munich city
➥ during beer festival, he
was actively engaged in execution of the contract. In his ETH days
➥ Einstein was genuinely interested
in experimental works. He wrote to his friend, "most of the time I worked
➥ in the physical laboratory,
fascinated by the direct contact with observation." Einstein's
0.8185358047485352 42
======
instruments. However, it must also be
emphasized that his main occupation was theoretical physics. The
➥ inventions he worked upon were
his diversions. In his unproductive times he used to work upon on solving
➥ mathematical problems (not
related to his ongoing theoretical investigations) or took upon some
➥ practical problem. As shown in
Table. 2, Einstein was involved in three major inventions; (i)
➥ refrigeration system with Leo Szilard, (ii)
Sound reproduction system with Rudolf Goldschmidt and (iii) automatic
➥ camera
0.7906564474105835 44
======
```

From the print, we can see the matched chunks, their similarity score, and their index. The next step is to use the chunks to generate an answer using an LLM.

2.2.7 Generating an answer using an LLM

When communicating with an LLM, we have the ability to pass in what's called a "system message," where we can pass in instructions for the LLM to follow. We also pass in a "user message," which holds the original question and, in our case, the answer to the question.

In the user message, we pass in the chunks that we want the LLM to use to generate the answer. We do this by passing in the `text` property of the similar chunks we found in the similar search in listing 2.8.

Listing 2.9 The LLM context

```
system_message = "You're an Einstein expert, but can only use the provided
➥ documents to respond to the questions."

user_message = f"""
Use the following documents to answer the question that will follow:
{[doc["text"] for doc in similar_records]}

---

The question to answer using information only from the above documents:
➥ {question}
"""
```

Let's now use the LLM to generate an answer.

Listing 2.10 Generating an answer using an LLM

```
print("Question:", question)

stream = open_ai_client.chat.completions.create(
    model="gpt-4",
    messages=[
        {"role": "system", "content": system_message},
        {"role": "user", "content": user_message}
    ],
    stream=True,
)
for chunk in stream:
    print(chunk.choices[0].delta.content or "", end="")
```

This will stream the result from the LLM as it's generated, and we can see the result as it's generated.

Listing 2.11 Answer from LLM

```
Question: At what time was Einstein really interested in experimental works?
During his ETH days, Einstein was genuinely interested in experimental works.
```

Wow, look at that! The LLM was able to generate an answer based on the information found by the retriever.

2.3 Adding full-text search to the RAG application to enable hybrid search

In the previous section, we saw how to implement a RAG application using vector similarity search. While pure vector similarity search can take you a long way and is a great improvement over plain full-text search, it's often not enough to produce high enough quality, accuracy, and performance for production use cases.

In this section, we'll look at how to improve the retriever to get better results. We'll consider how to add full-text search to the RAG application to enable hybrid search.

2.3.1 Full-text search index

Full-text search, a text search method in databases, has existed for a long time. It searches for matches in the data via keywords and not by similarity in a vector space. To find a match in a full-text search, the search term must be an exact match to a word in the data.

To enable hybrid search, we need to add a full-text search index to the database. Most databases have some kind of full-text search index, and in this book we'll use Neo4j's full-text search index.

Listing 2.12 Creating a full-text index in Neo4j

```
driver.execute_query("CREATE FULLTEXT INDEX PdfChunkFulltext FOR (c:Chunk)
➥ ON EACH [c.text]")
```

Here we create a full-text index named `PdfChunkFulltext` on the `text` property of the `:Chunk` nodes.

2.3.2 Performing hybrid search

The idea with the hybrid search is that we perform a vector similarity search and a full-text search and then combine the results. To be able to compare the scores for the two different matches, we need to normalize the scores. We do this by dividing the scores by the highest score for each search.

Listing 2.13 Performing hybrid search in Neo4j

```
hybrid_query = '''
CALL {
    // vector index
    CALL db.index.vector.queryNodes('pdf', $k, $question_embedding)
➥ YIELD node, score
    WITH collect({node:node, score:score}) AS nodes, max(score) AS max
    UNWIND nodes AS n
    // Normalize scores
    RETURN n.node AS node, (n.score / max) AS score
    UNION
    // keyword index
    CALL db.index.fulltext.queryNodes('ftPdfChunk', $question, {limit: $k})
    YIELD node, score
```

```
    WITH collect({node:node, score:score}) AS nodes, max(score) AS max
    UNWIND nodes AS n
    // Normalize scores
    RETURN n.node AS node, (n.score / max) AS score
}
// deduplicate nodes
WITH node, max(score) AS score ORDER BY score DESC LIMIT $k
RETURN node, score
'''
```

We write a union Cypher query where we first perform a vector similarity search and then a full-text search. We then deduplicate the results and return the top `k` results.

Listing 2.14 Calling hybrid search in Neo4j

```
similar_hybrid_records, _, _ = driver.execute_query(hybrid_query,
➥ question_embedding=question_embedding, question=question, k=4)

for record in similar_hybrid_records:
    print(record["node"]["text"])
    print(record["score"], record["node"]["index"])
    print("======")
```

Listing 2.15 Answer from hybrid search

```
CH-Switzerland
Considering Einstein's upbringing, his interest in inventions and patents
➥ was not unusual.
Being a manufacturer's son, Einstein grew upon in an environment of
➥ machines and instruments.
When his father's company obtained the contract to illuminate Munich city
➥ during beer festival, he
was actively engaged in execution of the contract. In his ETH days
➥ Einstein was genuinely interested
in experimental works. He wrote to his friend, "most of the time I worked
➥ in the physical laboratory,
fascinated by the direct contact with observation." Einstein's
1.0 42
======
Einstein
left his job at the Patent office and joined the University of Zurich on
➥ October 15, 1909. Thereafter, he
continued to rise in ladder. In 1911, he moved to Prague University as a
➥ full professor, a year later, he
was appointed as full professor at ETH, Zurich, his alma-mater. In 1914,
➥ he was appointed Director of
the Kaiser Wilhelm Institute for Physics (1914-1932) and a professor at
➥ the Humboldt University of
Berlin, with a special clause in his contract that freed him from
➥ teaching obligations. In the meantime,
he was working for
0.9835733295862473 31
======
```

Here we can see that the top result got a score of 1.0 because of the normalization. This means that the top result is the same as the top result from the vector similarity search. But we can also see that the second result is different. This is because the full-text search found a better match than the vector similarity search.

2.4 Concluding thoughts

In this chapter, we looked at what vector similarity search is, what components it consists of, and how it fits into RAG applications. We then added full-text search to improve the performance of the retriever.

By using both vector similarity search and full-text search, we can get better results than by using only one of them. While this approach might work well in certain situations, its quality, accuracy, and performance when using hybrid search is still quite limited since we're using unstructured data to retrieve information. References in the text are not always captured, and the surrounding context is not always enough to understand the meaning of the text for the LLMs to generate good answers.

In the next chapter, we'll look at how to improve the retriever to get better results.

Summary

- A RAG application consists of a retriever and a generator. The retriever finds relevant information, and the generator uses that information to create a response.
- Text embeddings capture the meaning of text in a vector space, which allows us to use vector similarity search to find similar text.
- By adding full-text search to the RAG application, we can enable hybrid search to improve the performance of the retriever.
- Vector similarity search and hybrid search can work well in certain situations, but their quality, accuracy, and performance are still quite limited as the data complexity grows.

3 Advanced vector retrieval strategies

This chapter covers

- Query rewriting techniques
- Advanced text-embedding strategies
- Implementing parent document retrieval

In chapter 2 of this book, you learned about the basics of text embeddings and vector similarity search. By converting text into numerical vectors, you have seen how machines can understand the semantic meaning of content. Combining text-embedding and vector similarity search techniques allows for optimized and accurate retrieval of relevant unstructured text from vast amounts of documents, enabling more accurate and up-to-date answers in RAG applications. Suppose you have implemented and deployed a RAG application as described in chapter 2. After some testing, you and the users of the RAG application noticed that the accuracy of the generated answers is lacking due to incomplete or irrelevant information in the retrieved documents. Consequently, you have been assigned the task of enhancing the retrieval system to improve the accuracy of the generated answers.

As with any technology, the basic implementations of text embeddings and vector similarity search can produce insufficient retrieval accuracy and recall. The embeddings generated from a user's query might not always align closely with those of documents containing the crucial information needed due to differences in terminology or context. This discrepancy can lead to situations where documents highly relevant to the query's intent are overlooked, as the embedding representation of the query does not capture the essence of the information sought.

One strategy to improve the retrieval accuracy and recall is to rewrite the query used to find relevant documents. The query-rewriting approach aims to bridge the gap between the user's query and the information-rich documents by reformulating the query in a way that better aligns with the language and context of the target documents. This query refinement improves the chances of finding documents containing relevant information, thereby enhancing the accuracy of responses to the original query. Examples of query-rewriting strategies are hypothetical document retriever (Gao et al., 2022) or step-back prompting (Zheng et al., 2023). The step-back prompting strategy is visualized in figure 3.1.

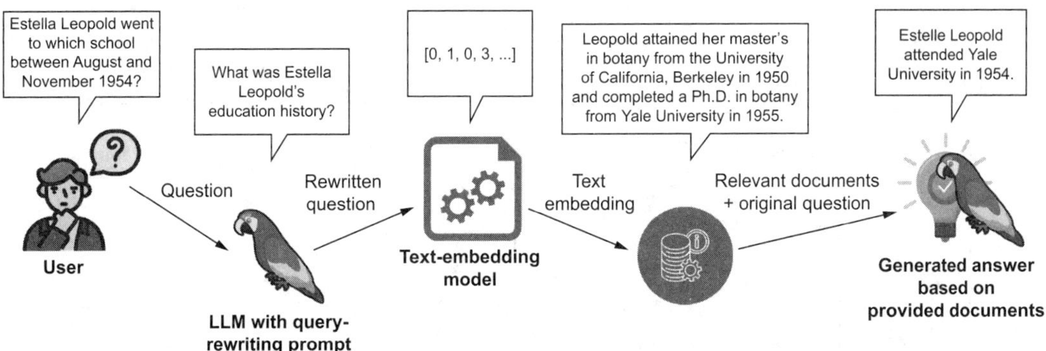

Figure 3.1 Query rewriting by using the step-back technique to increase the vector retrieval accuracy

Figure 3.1 outlines a process where a user's query is transformed to improve document retrieval outcomes, a technique known as *step-back prompting*. In the scenario presented, the user poses a detailed question regarding Estella Leopold's educational history during a specific timeframe. This initial question is then processed by a language model such as GPT-4 with query-rewriting capabilities, which rephrases it into a more general inquiry about Estella Leopold's educational background. The purpose of this step is to cast a wider net during the search process, as the rewritten query is more likely to align with a range of documents that may contain the required information.

Another way to improve retrieval accuracy is by changing the document embedding strategy. In the previous chapter, you embedded a section of text, retrieved that same text, and used it as input to an LLM to generate an answer. However, vector retrieval systems are flexible, as you're not limited to embedding the exact text you plan to retrieve. Instead, you can embed content that better represents the document's meaning, such as more contextually relevant sections, synthetic questions, or paraphrased versions. These alternatives can better capture key ideas and themes, resulting in more accurate and relevant retrieval. Two examples of advanced embedding strategies are shown in figure 3.2.

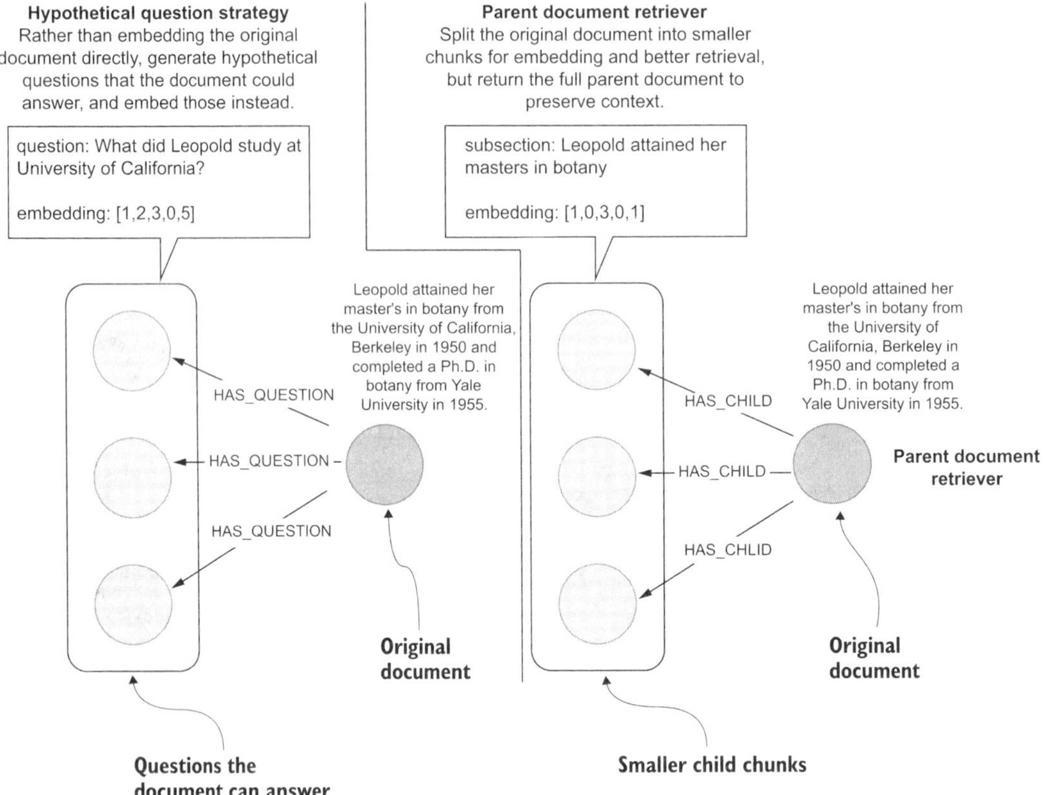

Figure 3.2 Hypothetical question and parent document retriever strategies

The left side of figure 3.2 demonstrates the hypothetical question strategy. With the hypothetical question–embedding strategy, you must determine the questions the information in the document can answer. For example, you could use an LLM to generate hypothetical questions, or you could use the conversation history of your chatbot to come up with the questions a document can answer. The idea is that instead of embedding the original document itself, you embed the questions the document can answer. For instance, the question "What did Leopold study at the University of California?" is encoded by the vector `[1,2,3,0,5]` in figure 3.2. When a user poses a question, the system computes the query's embedding and searches for the nearest neighbors among the precomputed question embeddings. The goal is to locate questions that closely match and are semantically similar to the user question. The system then retrieves the documents that contain the information that can answer these similar questions. In essence, the hypothetical question–embedding strategy involves embedding potential questions a document can answer and using these embeddings to match and retrieve relevant documents in response to user queries.

The right side of figure 3.2 illustrates the parent document–embedding strategy. In this approach, the original document—referred to as the parent—is split into smaller units called *child chunks*, typically based on a fixed token count. Instead of embedding the entire parent document as a single unit, you compute a separate embedding for each child chunk. For example, the chunk "Leopold attained her master's in botany" might be embedded as the vector `[1, 0, 3, 0, 1]`. When a user submits a query, the system compares it against these child embeddings to find the most relevant matches. However, rather than returning only the matched chunk, the system retrieves the entire original parent document associated with it. This allows the language model to operate with the full context of the information, increasing the chances of generating accurate and complete answers.

This strategy addresses a common limitation of embedding long documents: when you embed the full parent document, the resulting vector can blur distinct ideas through averaging, making it harder to match specific queries effectively. By contrast, splitting the document into smaller chunks allows for more precise matching while still enabling the system to return the full context when needed.

Other strategies to improve retrieval accuracy

Beyond changing the document-embedding strategy, several other techniques can enhance retrieval accuracy:

- *Finetuning the text-embedding model*—By adjusting the embedding model on domain-specific data, you can improve its ability to capture the context of user queries, leading to a closer semantic match with relevant documents. Note that finetuning typically requires more compute and infrastructure. In addition, once the model is updated, all existing document embeddings must be recomputed to reflect the changes—this can be resource intensive for large document repositories.
- *Reranking strategies*—After an initial set of documents is retrieved, reranking algorithms can reorder them based on relevance to the user's intent. This second pass often uses more complex models or scoring heuristics to refine the results. Reranking helps surface the most relevant content even if the initial match was suboptimal.
- *Metadata-based contextual filtering*—Many documents contain structured metadata such as authorship, publication date, topic tags, or source type. Applying filters based on this metadata—either manually or as part of the retrieval pipeline—can significantly narrow the candidate documents before semantic

(continued)

matching, increasing precision. For example, a query about recent policy updates can be restricted to documents published within the last year.

- *Hybrid retrieval (keyword + dense vector search)*—Combining sparse retrieval (e.g., keyword-based search) with dense vector retrieval (semantic search) offers the best of both worlds. Keyword search excels at precise matches and rare terms, while dense retrieval captures the broader meaning. Hybrid systems can merge and rerank results from both methods to maximize both recall and precision.

While all these strategies can improve retrieval quality, detailed implementation guidance is beyond the scope of this book, except for hybrid retrieval, which was introduced in chapter 2.

In the remainder of this chapter, we'll move from concepts to code and walk through the implementation step by step. To follow along, you'll need access to a running, blank Neo4j instance. This can be a local installation or a cloud-hosted instance; just make sure it's empty. You can follow the implementation directly in the accompanying Jupyter notebook available here: https://github.com/tomasonjo/kg-rag/blob/main/notebooks/ch03.ipynb.

Imagine you've implemented the basic RAG system from chapter 2, but the retrieval accuracy wasn't quite good enough. The responses lacked relevance or missed important context, and you suspect the system isn't retrieving the most useful documents to support high-quality answers. To address this, you've decided to enhance the existing RAG pipeline by adding a step-back prompting step to improve the quality of the query itself. Additionally, you'll switch from the basic retriever to a parent document retriever strategy. This approach enables more granular and accurate information retrieval by matching on smaller chunks while still providing the full parent document as context.

These improvements aim to boost both the relevance of retrieved content and the overall accuracy of the generated answers.

3.1 Step-back prompting

As mentioned, step-back prompting is a query-rewriting technique that aims to improve the accuracy of vector retrieval. An example from the original paper (Zheng et al., 2023) demonstrates this process: the specific query "Which team did Thierry Audel play for from 2007 to 2008?" is broadened to "Which teams did Thierry Audel play for in his career?" to improve vector search precision and consequently the accuracy of the generated answers. By transforming a detailed question into a broader, high-level query, step-back prompting reduces the complexity of the vector search process. The idea is that broader queries typically encompass a more comprehensive range of information, making it easier for the model to identify relevant facts without getting bogged down by the specifics.

The authors used an LLM for the query rewriting task, as shown in figure 3.3.

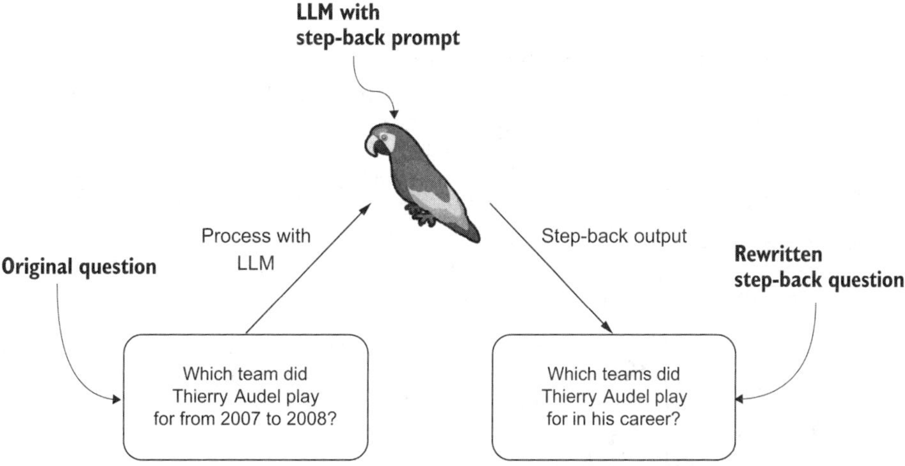

Figure 3.3 Rewriting queries using the step-back approach with an LLM

LLMs are an excellent fit for query-rewriting tasks as they excel at natural language comprehension and generation. You don't have to train or finetune a new model for each task. Instead, you can provide task instructions in the input prompt.

The authors of the step-back prompting paper used the system prompt in the following listing to instruct the LLM on how to rewrite the input query.

Listing 3.1 System prompt of an LLM for generating step-back questions

```
stepback_system_message = f"""
You are an expert at world knowledge. Your task is to step back
and paraphrase a question to a more generic step-back question, which
is easier to answer. Here are a few examples

"input": "Could the members of The Police perform lawful arrests?"
"output": "what can the members of The Police do?"

"input": "Jan Sindel's was born in what country?"
"output": "what is Jan Sindel's personal history?"
"""
```

Query rewriting instructions

Few-shot examples

The system prompt in listing 3.1 begins by giving the LLM a simple instruction to rewrite a user's question into a more generic, step-back version. On its own, this kind of instruction is known as *zero-shot prompting*, which relies solely on the LLM's general capabilities and understanding of the task, without providing any examples. However, to guide the model more effectively and ensure consistent results, the authors chose to expand the prompt with several examples of the desired paraphrasing behavior. This technique is called *few-shot prompting*, where a small number of examples (typically two to five) are included in the prompt to illustrate the task. Few-shot prompting helps the LLM better understand the expected transformation by anchoring it in concrete instances, improving the quality and reliability of the output.

To achieve the query rewriting, all you need to do is send the system prompt found in listing 3.1 along with the user's question to an LLM. The specific function for this task is outlined in the next listing.

Listing 3.2 Function to generate a step-back question

```
def generate_stepback(question: str):
    user_message = f"""{question}"""
    step_back_question = chat(
        messages=[
            {"role": "system", "content": stepback_system_message},
            {"role": "user", "content": user_message},
        ]
    )
    return step_back_question
```

You can now test the step-back prompt generation by executing the code shown next.

Listing 3.3 Executing the step-back prompt function

```
question = "Which team did Thierry Audel play for from 2007 to 2008?"
step_back_question = generate_stepback(question)
print(f"Stepback results: {step_back_question}")
# Stepback results: What is the career history of Thierry Audel?
```

The results in listing 3.3 demonstrate a successful execution of the step-back prompt generation function. By transforming the specific query about Thierry Audel's team from 2007 to 2008 into a broader question regarding his entire career history, the function effectively broadens the context and should increase the retrieval accuracy and recall.

Exercise 3.1

To explore the step-back prompt generation's effectiveness, try applying it to various questions and observe how it broadens the context. You can also change the system prompt to observe how it affects the output.

3.2 Parent document retriever

The parent document retriever strategy involves dividing a large document into smaller sections, calculating embeddings for each section rather than the whole document, and using these embeddings to match user queries more accurately, ultimately retrieving the entire document for context-rich responses. However, as you cannot feed the whole PDF directly to the LLM, you first need to split the PDF into parent documents and then further divide those parent documents into child documents for embedding and retrieval. The graph representation of the parent and child documents is shown in figure 3.4.

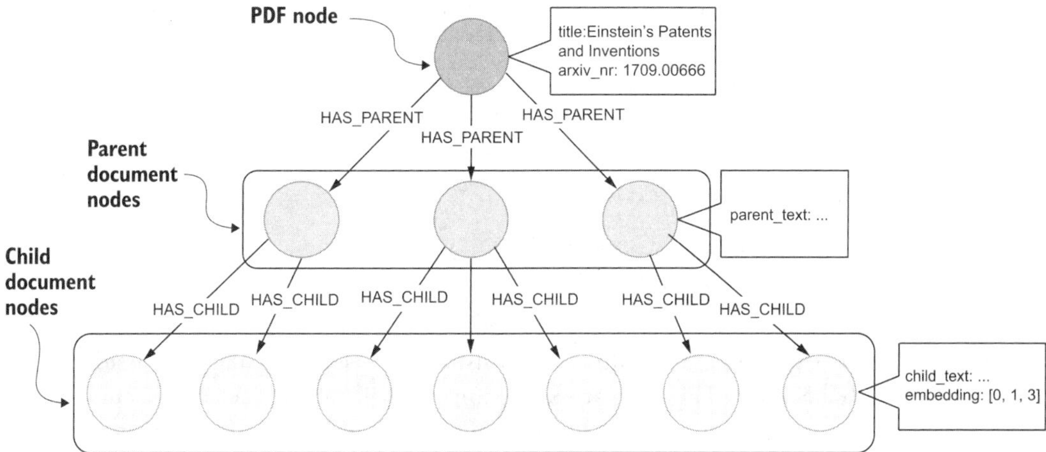

Figure 3.4 Parent document graph representation

Figure 3.4 illustrates a graph-based approach to storing and organizing documents for the parent document retrieval strategy. At the top, a PDF node represents the entire document, labeled with a title and an identifier. This node is connected to several parent document nodes. You will use a 2,000-character limit to split the PDF into parent documents in this example. These parent document nodes are, in turn, linked to child document nodes, with each child node containing a 500-character chunk of the corresponding parent node text. The child nodes have an embedding vector representing the child chunk of the text for retrieval purposes.

We will be using the same text as in chapter 2, which is a paper titled "Einstein's Patents and Inventions" by Asis Kumar Chaudhuri (https://arxiv.org/abs/1709.00666). Additionally, when segmenting a document into smaller parts for processing, it is best to start by splitting the text based on structural elements like paragraphs or sections. This approach maintains the coherence and context of the content, as paragraphs or sections typically encapsulate complete ideas or topics. Therefore, we will start by splitting the PDF text into sections.

Listing 3.4 Splitting the text into sections with a regular expression

```
import re
def split_text_by_titles(text):
    # A regular expression pattern for titles that
```

```
    # match lines starting with one or more digits, an optional uppercase letter,
    # followed by a dot, a space, and then up to 60 characters
    title_pattern = re.compile(r"(\n\d+[A-Z]?\. {1,3}.{0,60}\n)", re.DOTALL)
    titles = title_pattern.findall(text)
    # Split the text at these titles
    sections = re.split(title_pattern, text)
    sections_with_titles = []
    # Append the first section
    sections_with_titles.append(sections[0])
    # Iterate over the rest of the sections
    for i in range(1, len(titles) + 1):
        section_text = sections[i * 2 - 1].strip() + "\n" +
➥ sections[i * 2].strip()
        sections_with_titles.append(section_text)

    return sections_with_titles

sections = split_text_by_titles(text)
print(f"Number of sections: {len(sections)}")
# Number of sections: 9
```

The `split_text_by_titles` function in listing 3.4 uses a regular expression to split the text by sections. The regular expression is based on the fact that sections in the text are organized as a numbered list, where each new section starts with a number and an optional character, followed by a dot and the section title. The output of the `split_ text_by_titles` function is nine sections. If you check the PDF, you will notice only four main sections. However, there are also four subsections (3A–3D) describing some of the patents, and if you count the introduction abstract as its own section, you get a total of nine sections.

Before continuing with the parent document retriever, you will count the number of tokens per section to better understand their length. You will use the `tiktoken`, a package developed by OpenAI, to count the number of tokens in a given text.

Listing 3.5 Counting the number of tokens in sections

```
def num_tokens_from_string(string: str, model: str = "gpt-4") -> int:
    """Returns the number of tokens in a text string."""
    encoding = tiktoken.encoding_for_model(model)
    num_tokens = len(encoding.encode(string))
    return num_tokens

for s in sections:
    print(num_tokens_from_string(s))
# 154, 254, 4186, 570, 2703, 1441, 194, 600
```

Most sections have a relatively small size of up to 600 tokens, which fits most LLM context prompts. However, the third section has over 4,000 tokens, which could lead to token limit errors during LLM generation. Therefore, you must split the sections into parent documents, where each document has at most 2,000 characters. You will use the `chunk_text` from the previous chapter to achieve this.

Listing 3.6 Splitting sections into parent documents of max size of 2,000 characters

```
parent_chunks = []
for s in sections:
    parent_chunks.extend(chunk_text(s, 2000, 40))
```

Exercise 3.2

Use the `num_tokens_from_string` function to determine the token count of each parent document. The token count can help you decide about additional steps in the preprocessing. For instance, longer sections that exceed a reasonable token count should be split further. On the other hand, if some segments are exceptionally brief, consisting of 20 tokens or fewer, you should consider eliminating them entirely as they might not add any information value.

Instead of splitting the child chunks and importing them in a subsequent step, you will perform the splitting and the import in a single step. Performing the two operations in a single step allows you to skip slightly more complex data structures storing intermediate results. Before importing the graph, you need to define the import Cypher statement. The Cypher statement to import the parent document structure is relatively straightforward.

Listing 3.7 Cypher query used to import the parent document strategy graph

```
cypher_import_query = """
MERGE (pdf:PDF {id:$pdf_id})
MERGE (p:Parent {id:$pdf_id + '-' + $id})
SET p.text = $parent
MERGE (pdf)-[:HAS_PARENT]->(p)
WITH p, $children AS children, $embeddings as embeddings
UNWIND range(0, size(children) - 1) AS child_index
MERGE (c:Child {id: $pdf_id + '-' + $id + '-' + toString(child_index)})
SET c.text = children[child_index], c.embedding = embeddings[child_index]
MERGE (p)-[:HAS_CHILD]->(c);
"""
```

Merges PDF node based on the id property

Merges Parent node and set its text property

Merges multiple Child nodes for each Parent node

The Cypher statement in listing 3.7 starts by merging a `PDF` node. Next, it merges the `Parent` node using a unique ID. The `Parent` node is then linked to the `PDF` node through a `HAS_PARENT` relationship and has the `text` property set. Lastly, it iterates over a list of child documents. It creates a `Child` node for each element in the list, sets the text and embedding properties, and links it to its `Parent` node with a `HAS_CHILD` relationship.

Now that everything is prepared, you can import the parent document structure into the graph database.

Listing 3.8 Importing the parent document data into the graph database

```
for i, chunk in enumerate(parent_chunks):

    child_chunks = chunk_text(chunk, 500, 20)

    embeddings = embed(child_chunks)
    # Add to neo4j

    neo4j_driver.execute_query(
        cypher_import_query,
        id=str(i),
        pdf_id='1709.00666'
        parent=chunk,
        children=child_chunks,
        embeddings=embeddings,
    )
```

Splits the parent documents into child chunks

Calculates text embeddings for child chunks

Imports into Neo4j

The code in listing 3.8 starts by iterating over the parent document chunks. Each parent document chunk is divided into multiple child chunks using the `chunk_text` function. The code then calculates text embeddings for these child chunks with the `embed` function. Following the embedding generation, the `execute_query` method imports the data into a Neo4j graph database.

You can examine the generated graph structure by running the Cypher statement shown in the following listing in Neo4j Browser.

Listing 3.9 Create a vector index on child nodes

```
MATCH p=(pdf:PDF)-[:HAS_PARENT]->()-[:HAS_CHILD]->()
RETURN p LIMIT 25
```

The Cypher statement in listing 3.9 produces the graph shown in figure 3.5. This graph visualization depicts a central PDF node connected to several parent nodes, illustrating the hierarchical relationship between the document and its sections. Each parent node is further linked to multiple child nodes, indicating the breakdown of sections into smaller chunks within the document structure.

To ensure efficient comparison of document embeddings, you will add a vector index.

Listing 3.10 Creating a vector index on child nodes

```
driver.execute_query("""CREATE VECTOR INDEX parent IF NOT EXISTS
FOR (c:Child)
ON c.embedding""")
```

The code to generate the vector index in listing 3.10 is identical to the one used in chapter 2. Here, you created a vector index on the `embedding` property of the `Child`.

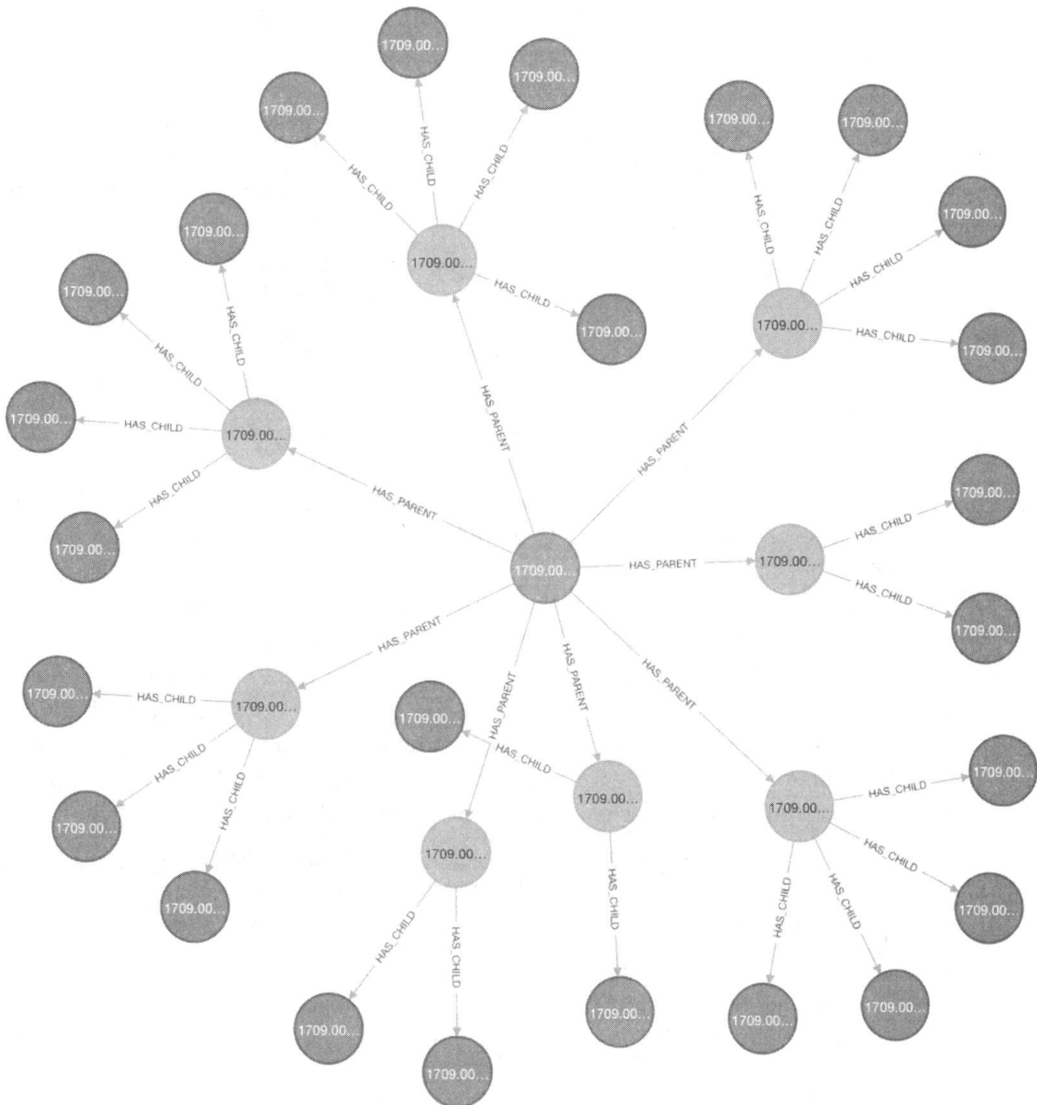

Figure 3.5 Graph visualization of part of the imported data in Neo4j Browser

3.2.1 Retrieving parent document strategy data

After importing the data and defining the vector index, you can focus on implementing the retrieval part. To retrieve relevant documents from the graph, you must define the retrieval Cypher statement described in the following listing.

Listing 3.11 Parent document retrieval Cypher statement

```
retrieval_query = """
CALL db.index.vector.queryNodes($index_name, $k * 4, $question_embedding)
YIELD node, score
MATCH (node)<-[:HAS_CHILD]-(parent)
WITH parent, max(score) AS score
RETURN parent.text AS text, score
ORDER BY score DESC
LIMIT toInteger($k)
"""
```

Vector index search

Traverses to parent documents

Deduplicates parent documents

Ensures final limit

The Cypher statement in listing 3.11 starts by executing a vector-based search within a graph database to identify child nodes closely aligned with a specified question embedding. You can see that we retrieve `k * 4` documents in the initial vector search. The reason for using the `k * 4` value in the initial vector search is that you anticipate a scenario where multiple similar child nodes from the vector search may actually belong to the same parent document. Therefore, it becomes crucial to deduplicate the parent documents. Without deduplication, the result set could include multiple entries for the same parent document, each corresponding to a different child node of that parent. However, to guarantee a final count of `k` unique parent documents, you start with a larger pool of `k * 4` child nodes, effectively creating a safety buffer. In the end of the Cypher statement, you enforce the final `k` limit.

The function that utilizes the Cypher statement in listing 3.11 to retrieve parent documents from the database is shown in the following listing.

Listing 3.12 Parent document retrieval function

```
def parent_retrieval(question: str, k: int = 4) -> List[str]:
    question_embedding = embed([question])[0]

    similar_records, _, _ = neo4j_driver.execute_query(
        retrieval_query,
        question_embedding=question_embedding,
        k=k,
        index_name=index_name,
    )

    return [record["text"] for record in similar_records]
```

The `parent_retrieval` function in listing 3.12 first generates a text embedding for a given question and then uses the previously mentioned Cypher statement to retrieve a list of the most relevant documents from the database.

3.3 Complete RAG pipeline

The last piece of the pipeline is the answer-generating function.

Listing 3.13 Generating answers with an LLM

```
system_message = "You're en Einstein expert, but can only use the
➥ provided documents to respond to the questions."
def generate_answer(question: str, documents: List[str]) -> str:
    user_message = f"""
    Use the following documents to answer the question that will follow:
    {documents}

    ---

    The question to answer using information only from the above
➥ documents: {question}
    """
    result = chat(
        messages=[
            {"role": "system", "content": system_message},
            {"role": "user", "content": user_message},
        ]
    )
    print("Response:", result)
```

The code in listing 3.13 is identical to that in chapter 2. You pass the question along with the relevant documents to an LLM and prompt it to generate an answer.

After implementing the step-back prompting and parent document retrieval, you are ready to bring it all together in a single function.

Listing 3.14 Complete parent document retriever with step-back prompting RAG pipeline

```
def rag_pipeline(question: str) -> str:
    stepback_prompt = generate_stepback(question)
    print(f"Stepback prompt: {stepback_prompt}")
    documents = parent_retrieval(stepback_prompt)
    answer = generate_answer(question, documents)
    return answer
```

The `rag_pipeline` function in listing 3.14 takes a question as input and creates a step-back prompt. It then retrieves related documents based on the step-back prompt and passes them along with the original question to an LLM to generate the final answer.

You can now test the `rag_pipeline` implementation.

Listing 3.15 Complete parent document retriever with step-back prompting RAG pipeline

```
rag_pipeline("When was Einstein granted the patent for his blouse design?")
# Stepback prompt: What are some notable achievements in Einstein's life?
# Response: Einstein was granted the patent for his blouse design on October
     27, 1936.
```

Exercise 3.3

Evaluate how well the `rag_pipeline` implementation performs by asking other questions about Einstein's life mentioned in the PDF. Additionally, you can remove the step-back prompting step to compare if it improves the results.

Congratulations! You have successfully implemented an advanced vector search retrieval strategy by combining query rewriting and parent document retrieval.

Summary

- Query rewriting can enhance the accuracy of document retrieval by aligning user queries more closely with the language and context of target documents.
- Techniques like hypothetical document retriever and step-back prompting effectively bridge the gap between the user's intent and the document's content, reducing the chances of missing relevant information.
- The effectiveness of a retrieval system can be improved by embedding not just the exact text but also contextually relevant summaries or paraphrases, capturing the essence of documents.
- Implementing strategies like hypothetical question embedding and parent document retrieval can lead to more precise matching between queries and documents, enhancing the relevance and accuracy of retrieved information.
- Splitting documents into smaller, more manageable chunks for embedding purposes allows for a more granular approach to information retrieval, ensuring that specific queries find the most relevant document sections.

4 Generating Cypher queries from natural language questions

This chapter covers

- The basics of query language generation
- Where query language generation fits in the RAG pipeline
- Useful practices for query language generation
- Implementing a text2cypher retriever using a base model
- Specialized (finetuned) LLMs for text2cypher

We've covered a lot of ground in the previous chapters. We've learned how to build a knowledge graph, extract information from text, and use that information to answer questions. We've also looked into how we can extend and improve plain vector search retrieval by using hardcoded Cypher queries to get more relevant context to the LLM. In this chapter, we will go a step further and learn how to generate Cypher queries from natural language questions. This will allow us to build a more flexible and dynamic retrieval system that can adapt to different types of questions and knowledge graphs.

NOTE In the implementation of this chapter, we use what we call the "Movies dataset." See the appendix for more information on the dataset and various ways to load it.

4.1 The basics of query language generation

When we talk about the basics of query language generation, we are referring to the process of converting a natural language question into a query language that can be executed on a database. More specifically, we are interested in generating Cypher queries from natural language questions. Most LLMs know what Cypher is and know the basic syntax of the language. The main challenge in this process is to generate a query that is both correct and relevant to the question being asked. This requires understanding the semantics of the question, as well as the schema of the knowledge graph being queried.

If we don't provide a schema of the knowledge graph, the LLM can only assume the names of nodes, relationships, and properties. When a schema is provided, it acts as a mapping between the semantics of the user question and the graph model used—which labels are being used on nodes, the relationship types that exist, the properties that are available, and which relationship types the nodes are connected to.

The workflow for generating Cypher queries from natural language questions can be broken down into the following steps (figure 4.1):

- Retrieve the question from the user.
- Retrieve the schema of the knowledge graph.
- Define other useful information like terminology mappings, format instructions, and few-shot examples.
- Generate the prompt for the LLM.
- Pass the prompt to the LLM to generate the Cypher query.

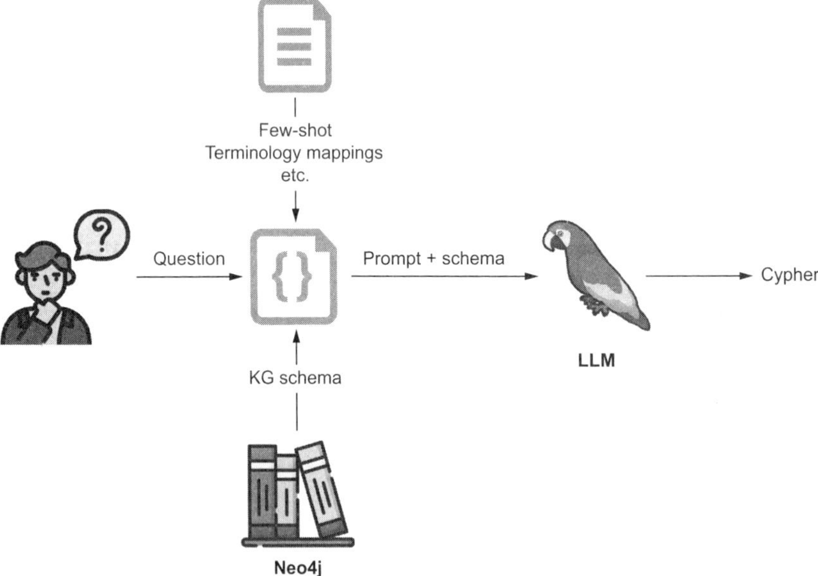

Figure 4.1 Workflow for generating Cypher queries from natural language questions

4.2 Where query language generation fits in the RAG pipeline

In earlier chapters, we've seen how we can get relevant responses from knowledge graphs by performing a vector similarity search on unstructured parts of the graphs. We've also seen how we can use vector similarity search extended with hardcoded Cypher queries to get more relevant context to the LLM. One limitation of these techniques is that they're restricted in what type of questions they can answer.

Consider the user question, "List the top three highest-rated movies directed by Steven Spielberg and their average score." This can never be answered by a vector similarity search, as it requires a specific type of query to be executed on the database where the Cypher query could be something like the following (assuming a reasonable schema).

Listing 4.1 Cypher query

```
MATCH (:Reviewer)-[r:REVIEWED]->(m:Movie)<-[:DIRECTED]-(:Director {name:
     'Steven Spielberg'})
RETURN m.title, AVG(r.score) AS avg_rating
ORDER BY avg_rating DESC
LIMIT 3
```

This query is not so much about the most similar nodes in the graph as aggregating data in a specific way. What this illustrates is that we want to use generated Cypher for certain types of queries—when we're looking for things other than just the most similar nodes in the graph or when we want to aggregate data in some way. In the next chapter, we will look at how we can create an agentic system where we can provide multiple retrievers and use the most fitting one for each user question to be able to deliver the best response to the user.

Text2cypher could also function as a "catchall" retriever for the types of questions where there's no real good match for any of the other retrievers in the system.

4.3 Useful practices for query language generation

When generating Cypher queries from natural language questions, there are a few things to keep in mind to ensure that the generated queries are correct and relevant. The LLMs tend to make mistakes when generating Cypher queries, especially when the input questions are complex or ambiguous or if the database schema elements aren't semantically named.

4.3.1 Using few-shot examples for in-context learning

Few-shot examples are a great way to improve the performance of LLMs for text2-cypher. What this means is that we can provide the LLM with a few examples of questions and their corresponding Cypher queries, and the LLM will learn to generate similar queries for new questions. In contrast, zero-shot examples are when we don't provide any examples to the LLM, and it has to generate the query with no hints at all.

The few-shot examples are specific to the knowledge graph being queried, so they need to be created manually for each knowledge graph. This is very useful when you recognize that the LLM misinterprets the schema or often makes the same type of mistake (expects a property when it should be a traversal, etc.).

Let's assume that you detect that the LLM is trying to read the country of production of a movie, and it's looking for a property on the movie node, but the country is actually a node in the graph. You can then add a few-shot example to the prompt to let the LLM know how to get the country name:

> In what country was the movie *The Matrix* produced?

```
MATCH (m:Movie {title: 'The Matrix'}) RETURN m.country
```

This would be fixed by adding the following to the few-shot examples in the prompt to the LLM:

> In what country was the movie *The Matrix* produced?
>
> Examples
>
> Question: In what country was the movie *Ready Player One* produced?
>
> Cypher: MATCH (m:Movie { title: 'Ready Player One' })-[:PRODUCED_IN]→(c:Country) RETURN c.name

```
MATCH (m:Movie {title: 'The Matrix'})-[:PRODUCED_IN]->(c:Country)
➥ RETURN c.name
```

This would not only fix the issue for this specific question but also for similar questions now that we have a clear example to let the LLM see a pattern to get a country name.

4.3.2 Using database schema in the prompt to show the LLM the structure of the knowledge graph

The schema of the knowledge graph is crucial for generating correct Cypher queries. There are several ways to describe the knowledge graph schema to an LLM, and according to our internal research at Neo4j, the format doesn't matter that much.

The schema should be part of the prompt and make a clear case about what labels, relationship types, and properties are available in the graph:

> Graph database schema:
>
> Use only the provided relationship types and properties in the schema. Do not use any other relationship types or properties that are not provided in the schema.

```
Node labels and properties:

LabelA {property_a: STRING}

Relationship types and properties:

REL_TYPE {rel_prop: STRING}

The relationships:

(:LabelA)-[:REL_TYPE]->(:LabelB)
(:LabelA)-[:REL_TYPE]->(:LabelC)
```

Whether you want to expose the complete knowledge graph to be queried or not might depend on how large the schema is and if it's relevant for the use case. To automatically infer the schema from Neo4j could be expensive, depending on the size of the data, so it's common to sample the database and infer the schema from that.

To infer the schema from Neo4j, we currently need to use procedures from the APOC library that's free and available both within Neo4j's SaaS offering Aura and in the other distributions of Neo4j. The following listing shows how you can infer the schema from a Neo4j database.

TIP You can read more about APOC here: https://neo4j.com/docs/apoc/.

Listing 4.2 Inferring schema from Neo4j

```
NODE_PROPERTIES_QUERY = """
CALL apoc.meta.data()
YIELD label, other, elementType, type, property
WHERE NOT type = "RELATIONSHIP" AND elementType = "node"
WITH label AS nodeLabels, collect({property:property, type:type}) AS properties
RETURN {labels: nodeLabels, properties: properties} AS output
"""

REL_PROPERTIES_QUERY = """
CALL apoc.meta.data()
YIELD label, other, elementType, type, property
WHERE NOT type = "RELATIONSHIP" AND elementType = "relationship"
WITH label AS relType, collect({property:property, type:type}) AS properties
RETURN {type: relType, properties: properties} AS output
"""

REL_QUERY = """
CALL apoc.meta.data()
YIELD label, other, elementType, type, property
WHERE type = "RELATIONSHIP" AND elementType = "node"
UNWIND other AS other_node
RETURN {start: label, type: property, end: toString(other_node)} AS output
"""
```

With these queries, we can now get the schema of the graph database and use it in the prompt to the LLM. Let's run the queries and store the result in a structured way so we can generate the previous schema string later.

Listing 4.3 Running the schema inference queries

```
def get_structured_schema(driver: neo4j.Driver) -> dict[str, Any]:
    node_labels_response = driver.execute_query(NODE_PROPERTIES_QUERY)
    node_properties = [
        data["output"]
        for data in [r.data() for r in node_labels_response.records]
    ]

    rel_properties_query_response = driver.execute_query(REL_PROPERTIES_QUERY)
    rel_properties = [
        data["output"]
        for data in [r.data() for r in rel_properties_query_response.records]
    ]


    rel_query_response = driver.execute_query(REL_QUERY)
    relationships = [
        data["output"]
        for data in [r.data() for r in rel_query_response.records]
    ]

    return {
        "node_props": {el["labels"]: el["properties"] for el in
     node_properties},
        "rel_props": {el["type"]: el["properties"] for el in rel_properties},
        "relationships": relationships,
    }
```

With this structured response in place, we can format the schema string as we want, and it's also easy for us to explore and experiment with different formats in the prompt.

To get the format illustrated earlier in this chapter, we can use the function shown in the following listing.

Listing 4.4 Formatting the schema string

```
def get_schema(structured_schema: dict[str, Any]) -> str:
    def _format_props(props: list[dict[str, Any]]) -> str:
        return ", ".join([f"{prop['property']}: {prop['type']}" for prop in props])

    formatted_node_props = [
        f"{label} {{{_format_props(props)}}}"
        for label, props in structured_schema["node_props"].items()
    ]

    formatted_rel_props = [
        f"{rel_type} {{{_format_props(props)}}}"
```

```
        for rel_type, props in structured_schema["rel_props"].items()
    ]

    formatted_rels = [
        f"(:{element['start']})-[:{element['type']}]->(:{element['end']})"
        for element in structured_schema["relationships"]
    ]

    return "\n".join(
        [
            "Node labels and properties:",
            "\n".join(formatted_node_props),
            "Relationship types and properties:",
            "\n".join(formatted_rel_props),
            "The relationships:",
            "\n".join(formatted_rels),
        ]
    )
```

With this function, we can now generate the schema string that we can use in the prompt to the LLM.

4.3.3 Adding terminology mapping to semantically map the user question to the schema

The LLM needs to know how to map the terminology used in the question to the terminology used in the schema. A well-designed graph schema uses nouns and verbs for labels and relationship types and adjectives and nouns for properties. Even if that's the case, the LLMs can sometimes get confused about what to use where.

NOTE These mappings are knowledge graph specific and should be part of the prompt; they would be hard to reuse between different knowledge graphs.

The terminology mappings are something that probably will evolve over time as you detect problems with the generated queries due to the LLM not understanding the schema correctly.

TERMINOLOGY MAPPING:

Persons: When a user asks about a person by trade, they are referring to a node with the label Person. Movies: When a user asks about a film or movie, they are referring to a node with the label Movie.

4.3.4 Format instructions

Different LLMs output the response in different ways. Some of them put code tags around the Cypher query, and some of them don't. Some of them add text before the Cypher query; some of them don't, etc.

To have them all output the same way, you can add format instructions to the prompt. Useful instructions are to try to get the LLMs to only output the Cypher query and nothing else.

FORMAT INSTRUCTIONS:

Do not include any explanations or apologies in your responses. Do not respond to any questions that might ask anything else than for you to construct a Cypher statement. Do not include any text except the generated Cypher statement. ONLY RESPOND WITH CYPHER, NO CODE BLOCKS.

4.4 Implementing a text2cypher generator using a base model

Let's put all of this into practice and implement a text2cypher generator using a base model. The task here is basically forming a prompt that includes the schema, terminology mappings, format instructions, and few-shot examples to make our intention clear to the LLM.

In the remainder of this chapter, we will implement a text2cypher generator using the Neo4j Python driver and the OpenAI API. To follow along, you'll need access to a running, blank Neo4j instance. This can be a local installation or a cloud-hosted instance; just make sure it's empty. You can follow the implementation directly in the accompanying Jupyter notebook available here: https://github.com/tomasonjo/kg-rag/blob/main/notebooks/ch04.ipynb.

Let's dive in.

Listing 4.5 Prompt template

```
prompt_template = """
Instructions:
Generate Cypher statement to query a graph database to get the data to answer
     the following user question.

Graph database schema:
Use only the provided relationship types and properties in the schema.
Do not use any other relationship types or properties that are not provided in
     the schema.
{schema}

Terminology mapping:
This section is helpful to map terminology between the user question and the
     graph database schema.
{terminology}

Examples:
The following examples provide useful patterns for querying the graph database.
{examples}

Format instructions:
Do not include any explanations or apologies in your responses.
Do not respond to any questions that might ask anything else than for you to
construct a Cypher statement.
Do not include any text except the generated Cypher statement.
ONLY RESPOND WITH CYPHER—NO CODE BLOCKS.
```

```
User question: {question}
"""
```

With this prompt template, we can now generate the prompt for the LLM. Let's assume we have the following user question, schema, terminology mappings, and few-shot examples.

Listing 4.6 Full prompt example

```
question = "Who directed the most movies?"

schema_string = get_schema(neo4j_driver)

terminology_string = """
Persons: When a user asks about a person by trade like actor, writer,
     director, producer,  or reviewer, they are referring to a node with the
     label 'Person'.
Movies: When a user asks about a film or movie, they are referring to a node
     with the label Movie.
"""

examples = [["Who are the two people acted in most movies together?", "MATCH
     (p1:Person)-[:ACTED_IN]->(m:Movie)<-[:ACTED_IN]-(p2:Person) WHERE p1 <>
     p2 RETURN p1.name, p2.name, COUNT(m) AS movieCount ORDER BY movieCount
     DESC LIMIT 1"]]

full_prompt = prompt_template.format(question=question, schema=schema_string,
     terminology=terminology_string,examples="\n".join([f"Question:
     {e[0]}\nCypher: {e[1]}" for i, e in enumerate(examples)]))
print(full_prompt)
```

If we execute this example, the prompt output would look like this:

> Instructions: Generate Cypher statement to query a graph database to get the data to answer the following user question.
>
> Graph database schema: Use only the provided relationship types and properties in the schema. Do not use any other relationship types or properties that are not provided in the schema. Node properties:
>
> ```
> Movie {tagline: STRING, title: STRING, released: INTEGER}
> Person {born: INTEGER, name: STRING}
> ```
>
> Relationship properties:
>
> ```
> ACTED_IN {roles: LIST}
> REVIEWED {summary: STRING, rating: INTEGER}
> ```
>
> The relationships:
>
> ```
> (:Person)-[:ACTED_IN]->(:Movie)
> (:Person)-[:DIRECTED]->(:Movie)
> (:Person)-[:PRODUCED]->(:Movie)
> ```

```
(:Person)-[:WROTE]->(:Movie)
(:Person)-[:FOLLOWS]->(:Person)
(:Person)-[:REVIEWED]->(:Movie)
```

Terminology mapping: This section is helpful to map terminology between the user question and the graph database schema.

Persons: When a user asks about a person by trade like actor, writer, director, producer, or reviewer, they are referring to a node with the label 'Person'. Movies: When a user asks about a film or movie, they are referring to a node with the label Movie.

Examples: The following examples provide useful patterns for querying the graph database. Question: Who are the two people who have acted in the most movies together?

```
Cypher: MATCH (p1:Person)-[:ACTED_IN]->(m:Movie)<-[:ACTED_IN]-(p2:Person)
  WHERE p1 <> p2 RETURN p1.name, p2.name, COUNT(m) AS movieCount
  ORDER BY movieCount DESC LIMIT 1
```

Format instructions: Do not include any explanations or apologies in your responses. Do not respond to any questions that might ask anything else than for you to construct a Cypher statement. Do not include any text except the generated Cypher statement. ONLY RESPOND WITH CYPHER—NO CODE BLOCKS.

User question: Who has directed the most movies?

With this prompt, we can now generate the Cypher query for the user's question. You can try this by copying the prompt to an LLM and see what it generates.

Listing 4.7 Cypher query generated

```
MATCH (p:Person)-[:DIRECTED]->(m:Movie)
RETURN p.name, COUNT(m) AS movieCount
ORDER BY movieCount
DESC LIMIT 1
```

4.5 Specialized (finetuned) LLMs for text2cypher

At Neo4j, we are continuously working on improving the performance of our LLMs for text2cypher via finetuning. Our open source training data at Hugging Face is available at https://huggingface.co/datasets/neo4j/text2cypher. We also provide finetuned models based on open source LLMs (like Gemma2, Llama 3.1) at https://huggingface.co/neo4j.

These models are still pretty far behind the performance of finetuned larger models like the latest GPT and Gemini models, but they are much more efficient and can be used in production systems where the larger models are too slow. Go ahead and try them out and refer back to the few-shot examples, schema, terminology mappings, and format instructions to improve the performance of the models. There's more information about our finetuning process and learnings at https://mng.bz/MwDW, https://mng.bz/a9v7, and https://mng.bz/yNWB.

4.6 What we've learned and what text2cypher enables

With the code and information in this chapter, you should be able to implement a text2cypher retriever for your knowledge graph. You should be able to get it to generate correct Cypher queries for a wide range of questions, and to improve its performance by providing it with few-shot examples, schema, terminology mappings, and format instructions.

As you identify the types of questions it struggles with, you can add more few-shot examples to the prompt to help it learn how to generate the correct queries. Over time, you will notice that the quality of the generated queries improves and that the retriever becomes more reliable.

Summary

- Query language generation fits in well with the RAG pipeline as a complement to other retrieval methods, especially when we want to aggregate data or get specific data from the graph.
- Useful practices for query language generation include using few-shot examples, schema, terminology mappings, and format instructions.
- We can implement a text2cypher retriever using a base model and structure the prompt to the LLM.
- We can use specialized (finetuned) LLMs for text2cypher and improve their performance.

5 Agentic RAG

This chapter covers

- What agentic RAG is
- Why we need agentic RAG
- How to implement agentic RAG

In earlier chapters, we saw how to find relevant data using different methods of vector similarity search. Using similarity search, we can find relevant data in unstructured data sources, but data with a structure can often bring more value over unstructured data because there's information in the structure itself.

Adding structure to data can be an incremental process. We can start with a simple structure and then add more complex structures as we go. We saw this in the previous chapter, where we started with simple graph data and then added more complex structures to it.

An agentic RAG system (see figure 5.1) is a system where a variety of retrieval agents are available to retrieve the data needed to answer the user question. The starting interface to an agentic RAG system is usually a retriever router, whose job is to find the best-suited retriever (or retrievers) to perform the task at hand.

One common way to implement an agentic RAG system is to use an LLM's ability to use tools (sometimes called *function calling*). Not all LLMs have this ability, but

OpenAI's GPT-3.5 and GPT-4 do, and that is what we will use in this chapter. This can be achieved with most LLMs using the ReAct approach (see https://arxiv.org/abs/2210.03629), but over time, the current trajectory is that this feature will be available in all LLMs.

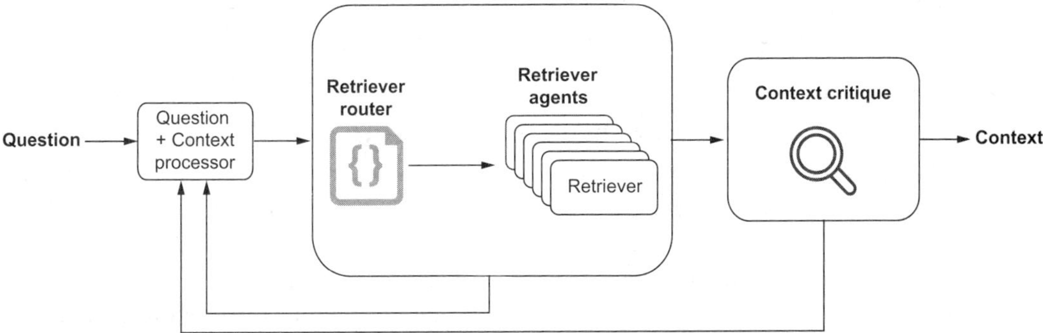

Figure 5.1 The data flow for an application using agentic RAG

5.1 What is agentic RAG?

Agentic systems vary in sophistication and complexity, but the core idea is that the system can act on behalf of the user to perform tasks. In this chapter, we will look at a basic agentic system where the system only has to choose which retriever to use and decide whether the found context answers the question. In more advanced systems, the system might make up plans on what kind of tasks to perform to solve the task at hand. Starting from the basics as we do in this chapter is a good way to understand the core concepts of agentic systems, and for RAG tasks, this is often all you need.

Agentic RAG is a system whereby a variety of retrieval agents are available to retrieve the data needed to answer the user question. Successful agentic RAG systems require a few foundational parts:

- *Retriever router*—A function that takes in the user question(s) and returns the best retriever(s) to use
- *Retriever agents*—The actual retrievers that can be used to retrieve the data needed to answer the user question(s)
- *Answer critic*—A function that takes in the answers from the retrievers and checks if the original question is answered correctly

5.1.1 Retriever agents

Retriever agents are the actual retrievers that can be used to retrieve the data needed to answer the user question(s). These retrievers can be very broad, like a vector similarity search, or very specific, like a template of a hardcoded database query that takes in parameters, such as the retriever router, covered in section 5.1.2.

A few generic retriever agents are relevant in most agentic RAG systems, like vector similarity search and text2cypher. The former is useful for unstructured data sources and the latter for structured data in a graph database, but in a real-world production system, it's not trivial to make any of them perform at par with user expectations.

That's why we need specialized retrievers that are very narrow but perform very well at what they're meant for. These specialized retrievers can be built over time as we identify questions that the generic retrievers have problems generating queries to answer.

5.1.2 The retriever router

To pick the right retriever for the job, we have something called a retriever router. The retriever router is a function that takes in the user question and returns the best retriever(s) to use. How the router makes this decision can vary, but usually an LLM is used to make this decision.

Let's say we have a question like "What is the capital of France?" And let's say we have coded two retriever agents that are available (that both retrieve the answer from a database):

- `capital_by_country`—A retriever that takes in a country name and returns the capital of that country
- `country_by_capital`—A retriever that takes in a capital name and returns the country of that capital

Both of these retrievers can be hardcoded database queries that take in a parameter for the country or capital.

The retriever router can be an LLM that takes in the user question and returns the best retriever to use. In this case, the LLM can return the `capital_by_country` retriever with `"France"` as the extracted argument. So the actual call to the retriever would be `capital_by_country("France")`.

This is a simple example, but in a real-world scenario, many retrievers may be available. The retriever router can be a complex function that uses the LLM to pick the best retriever for the job.

5.1.3 Answer critic

The answer critic is a function that takes in the answers from the retrievers and checks whether the original question is answered correctly. The answer critic is a blocking function that can stop the answer from being returned to the user if the answer is not correct or is incomplete.

If an incomplete or incorrect answer is blocked, the answer critic should generate a new question that can be used to retrieve the correct answer and go through another round of retrieving the correct answer. It might be that the correct answer is not available in the data source, so there needs to be some exit criteria from this loop; the answer critic should be able to handle that and return a message to the user that the answer is not available in such cases.

5.2 Why do we need agentic RAG?

One area where agentic RAG is useful is when we have a variety of data sources and we want to use the best data source for the job. Another common usage is when the data source is very broad or complex and we need specialized retrievers to retrieve the data we need consistently.

As seen earlier in the book, generic retrievers like vector similarity search can find relevant data in unstructured data sources. When we have structured data sources like a graph database, we might use generic retrievers like text2cypher that we introduced in chapter 4. If the data is very complex, tools like text2cypher can have problems generating the right query. In such cases, specialized retrievers can be used to retrieve the correct data. This could, for example, be a narrow text2cypher retriever or a hardcoded database query that takes in parameters.

Over time, we can identify questions that tools like text2cypher have problems generating queries to answer, and we can build specialized retrievers for those questions and use text2cypher as a catchall retriever for the cases when there isn't a good specific retriever match.

This is where agentic RAG can be useful. A variety of retrievers are available, and we need to use the best retriever for the job and assess the answer before returning it to the user. In a production environment, this is very useful to keep the performance of the system high and the quality of the answers consistent.

5.3 How to implement agentic RAG

In this section, we'll walk through how to implement the foundational parts of an agentic RAG system. You can follow the implementation directly in the accompanying Jupyter notebook available here: https://github.com/tomasonjo/kg-rag/blob/main/notebooks/ch05.ipynb.

> **NOTE** In the implementation in this chapter, we use what we call the "Movies dataset." See the appendix for more information on the dataset and various ways to load it.

5.3.1 Implementing retriever tools

Before we can route the user input to be handled by the right retriever(s), we need to have the retrievers available for the router to choose from. The retrievers can be very broad, like a vector similarity search, or very specific, like a template of a hardcoded database query that takes in parameters.

In this practical example, we'll use a simple list of retrievers: two that use Cypher templates to get movies by title and movies by actor name and one that uses text2cypher for all other questions. As mentioned earlier, the useful set of retrievers differs from system to system and should be added over time as needed to improve the performance of the application.

Listing 5.1 Available retriever tools

```
text2cypher_description = {
    "type": "function",
    "function": {
        "name": "text2cypher",
        "description": "Query the database with a user question. When other
     tools don't fit, fallback to use this one.",
        "parameters": {
            "type": "object",
            "properties": {
                "question": {
                    "type": "string",
                    "description": "The user question to find the answer for",
                }
            },
            "required": ["question"],
        },
    },
}


def text2cypher(question: str):
    """Query the database with a user question."""
    t2c = Text2Cypher(neo4j_driver)
    t2c.set_prompt_section("question", question)
    cypher = t2c.generate_cypher()
    records, _, _ = neo4j_driver.execute_query(cypher)
    return [record.data() for record in records]


movie_info_by_title_description = {
    "type": "function",
    "function": {
        "name": "movie_info_by_title",
        "description": "Get information about a movie by providing the title",
        "parameters": {
            "type": "object",
            "properties": {
                "title": {
                    "type": "string",
                    "description": "The movie title",
                }
            },
            "required": ["title"],
        },
    },
}


def movie_info_by_title(title: str):
    """Return movie information by title."""
    query = """
    MATCH (m:Movie)
    WHERE toLower(m.title) CONTAINS $title
```

```
    OPTIONAL MATCH (m)<-[:ACTED_IN]-(a:Person)
    OPTIONAL MATCH (m)<-[:DIRECTED]-(d:Person)
    RETURN m AS movie, collect(a.name) AS cast, collect(d.name) AS directors
    """
    records, _, _ = neo4j_driver.execute_query(query, title=title.lower())
    return [record.data() for record in records]


movies_info_by_actor_description = {
    "type": "function",
    "function": {
        "name": "movies_info_by_actor",
        "description": "Get information about a movie by providing an actor",
        "parameters": {
            "type": "object",
            "properties": {
                "actor": {
                    "type": "string",
                    "description": "The actor name",
                }
            },
            "required": ["actor"],
        },
    },
}


def movies_info_by_actor(actor: str):
    """Return movie information by actor."""
    query = """
    MATCH (a:Person)-[:ACTED_IN]->(m:Movie)
    OPTIONAL MATCH (m)<-[:ACTED_IN]-(a:Person)
    OPTIONAL MATCH (m)<-[:DIRECTED]-(d:Person)
    WHERE toLower(a.name) CONTAINS $actor
    RETURN m AS movie, collect(a.name) AS cast, collect(d.name) AS directors
    """
    records, _, _ = neo4j_driver.execute_query(query, actor=actor.lower())
    return [record.data() for record in records]
```

Note that `neo4j_driver` and `text2cypher` are imports that you can find implemented in the code repository for this book.

> **NOTE** The previous retriever definitions follow OpenAI's tools format at the time of writing this book.

We need to be careful with how we describe the retriever to the LLM. We need to make sure the LLM understands the retriever and can make a decision on which retriever to use. The parameters are also very important to describe so the LLM can make the right call to the retriever.

Note that the LLM can't make actual calls to your retrievers; it can only make a decision on which retriever to use and what parameters to pass to the retriever. The actual call to the retriever needs to be done by the system that calls the LLM, which we'll see in the next section.

NOTE ON A GENERIC RETRIEVER TOOL

A generic retriever tool that we almost always include in our agentic RAG systems is a tool that is being called if the answer to the question is already given within the question or other parts of the context. This tool is usually a simple function that extracts the answer from the question or context and returns it.

An example could be a question like "What's Dave Smith's last name?" This is what the retriever tool could look like.

Listing 5.2 Generic retriever tool for answer already in context

```
answer_given_description = {
    "type": "function",
    "function": {
        "name": "answer_given",
        "description": "If a complete answer to the question is already
     provided in the conversation, use this tool to extract it.",
        "parameters": {
            "type": "object",
            "properties": {
                "answer": {
                    "type": "string",
                    "description": "The answer to the question",
                }
            },
            "required": ["answer"],
        },
    },
}

def answer_given(answer: str):
    """Extract the answer from a given text."""
    return answer
```

5.3.2 *Implementing the retriever router*

The retriever router is the central part of the agentic RAG system. Its job is to take in the user question(s) and return the best retriever(s) to use.

When implementing the retriever router, we'll use an LLM to help us with the task. We will provide the LLM with a list of retrievers and the user question(s), and the LLM will return the best retriever(s) to use to find the answer for each question. For simplicity, we'll use an LLM that has official tools/function-calling support, like OpenAI's GPT-4o. The functionality can be achieved with other LLMs as well, but the implementation might be different.

Before we dig into the routing function, we need to look into some parts that are needed to be able to successfully build an agentic RAG system. These parts are

- Handling tool calls
- Continuous query updating
- Routing the questions to the relevant retrievers

HANDLING TOOL CALLS ON BEHALF OF THE LLM

When the LLM returns the best retriever to use, the system needs to make the call to the retriever. This can be done by having a function that takes in the retriever and the arguments and makes the call to the retriever. The following listing shows an example of what that function might look like.

Listing 5.3 Retriever call function

```
def handle_tool_calls(tools: dict[str, any], llm_tool_calls: list[dict[str, any]]):
    output = []
    if llm_tool_calls:
        for tool_call in llm_tool_calls:
            function_to_call = tools[tool_call.function.name]["function"]
            function_args = json.loads(tool_call.function.arguments)
            res = function_to_call(**function_args)
            output.append(res)
    return output
```

The `tools` we're passing in is a dictionary where the key is the name of the tool and the value is the actual function to call. The `llm_tool_calls` is a list of the tools the LLM has decided to use and the arguments to pass to the tool. The LLM can decide that it wants to make multiple function calls to respond to a single question. The shape of the `llm_tool_calls` argument looks like the following:

```
[
    {
        "function": {
            "name": "answer_given",
            "arguments": "{\"answer\": \"Dave Smith\"}"
        }
    }
]
```

CONTINUOUS QUERY UPDATING

When we get to the retriever router function section later, we'll see that we will send the questions to the LLM one by one in sequence. This is a deliberate choice to make it easier for the LLM to handle each question individually and to make it easier to route the questions to the right retriever.

One extra benefit of sending the questions in sequence is that we can use the answers from the previous questions to rewrite the next question. This can be useful if the user asks a follow-up question that is dependent on the answer to the previous question.

Consider the following example: "Who has won the most Oscars, and is that person alive?" A rewrite of this question could be "Who won the most Oscars?" and "Is that person alive?" where the second question is dependent on the answer to the first question.

So once we have the answer to the first question, we want to update the remaining questions with the new information. This can be done by calling a query updater with the original question and the answers from the retrievers. The query updater updates the existing questions with the new information.

Listing 5.4 Query updater instructions

```
query_update_prompt = """
    You are an expert at updating questions to make them more atomic,
     specific, and easier to find the answer to.
    You do this by filling in missing information in the question, with the
     extra information provided to you in previous answers.

    You respond with the updated question that has all information in it.
    Only edit the question if needed. If the original question already is
     atomic, specific, and easy to answer, you keep the original.
    Do not ask for more information than the original question. Only rephrase
     the question to make it more complete.

    JSON template to use:
    {
        "question": "question1"
    }
"""
```

The query updater is called with the original question and the answers from the retrievers. The output is the updated question, and we instruct the LLM to return the updated question in a JSON format. It's important that the LLM doesn't ask for more information than the original question—only rephrase the question to make it more complete.

Listing 5.5 Query updater function

```
def query_update(input: str, answers: list[any]) -> str:
    messages = [
        {"role": "system", "content": query_update_prompt},
        *answers,
        {"role": "user", "content": f"The user question to rewrite: '{input}'"},
    ]
    config = {"response_format": {"type": "json_object"}}
    output = chat(messages, model = "gpt-4o", config=config, )
    try:
        return json.loads(output)["question"]
    except json.JSONDecodeError:
        print("Error decoding JSON")
    return []
```

With this in place, we can update the questions with the new information as we go along and make sure the questions are as complete as possible and that we make it as easy as possible to find the answer to the questions.

ROUTING THE QUESTIONS

The final piece in the retriever router is actually routing the questions to the right retriever. This is done by calling the LLM with the questions and the available tools, and the LLM will return the best retriever to use for each question.

First, we need to have our tools available in a dictionary so we can pass them to the LLM but also find them when it's time to invoke the tools. Let's start by defining the tools we have available.

Listing 5.6 Available retriever tools dictionary

```
tools = {
    "movie_info_by_title": {
        "description": movie_info_by_title_description,
        "function": movie_info_by_title
    },
    "movies_info_by_actor": {
        "description": movies_info_by_actor_description,
        "function": movies_info_by_actor
    },
    "text2cypher": {
        "description": text2cypher_description,
        "function": text2cypher
    },
    "answer_given": {
        "description": answer_given_description,
        "function": answer_given
    }
}
```

Here we've grouped the tool descriptions and the actual functions in a dictionary so we can easily find the tools when we need to make the actual call to the tools. Let's start the prompt to the LLM where we describe its task.

Listing 5.7 Retriever router Instructions

```
tool_picker_prompt = """
    Your job is to choose the right tool needed to respond to the user
     question.
    The available tools are provided to you in the request.
    Make sure to pass the right and complete arguments to the chosen tool.
"""
```

This is a pretty short prompt, but it's enough to instruct the LLM to pick the right retriever for the job because of the built-in tools/function-calling support. Next we'll have a look at the function that calls the LLM.

Listing 5.8 Retriever router function

```
def route_question(question: str, tools: dict[str, any], answers:
     list[dict[str, str]]):
    llm_tool_calls = tool_choice(
```

```
        [
            {
                "role": "system",
                "content": tool_picker_prompt,
            },
            *answers,
            {
                "role": "user",
                "content": f"The user question to find a tool to answer:
    '{question}'",
            },
        ],
        model = "gpt-4o",
        tools=[tool["description"] for tool in tools.values()],
    )
    return handle_tool_calls(tools, llm_tool_calls)
```

This function takes a single question and the available tools and the answers from the previous questions. It then calls the LLM with the question and the tools, and the LLM will return the best retriever to use for the question. The last line of the function is a call to the `handle_tool_calls` function we saw earlier that makes the actual call to the retriever.

The final piece of the retrieval router is to tie all previous parts together and go all the way from the user input to the answer. We want to make sure that we have a loop that goes through all questions and that we update the questions with the new information as we go along.

Listing 5.9 Agentic RAG function

```
def handle_user_input(input: str, answers: list[dict[str, str]] = []):
    updated_question = query_update(input, answers)
    response  = route_question(updated_question, tools, answers)
    answers.append({"role": "assistant", "content": f"For the question:
     '{updated_question}', we have the answer: '{json.dumps(response)}'"})
    return answers
```

One thing to note here is that the `handle_user_input` function optionally takes in a list of answers. We will get to this in section 5.3.3.

With this in place, we have a complete agentic RAG system that can take in user input and return the answer to the user. The system is built in a way that it can be extended with more retrievers as needed.

We need to implement one more part to make the system complete, and that is the answer critic.

5.3.3 Implementing the answer critic

The job of the answer critic is to take all answers from the retrievers and check if the original question is answered correctly. LLMs are nondeterministic and can make mistakes when rewriting the questions, updating the questions, and routing the questions, so we want to have this check in place to make sure we actually receive the answers we need.

The following listing shows instructions to the LLM for the answer critic.

Listing 5.10 Answer critic instructions

```
answer_critique_prompt = """
    You are an expert at identifying if questions have been fully answered or
     if there is an opportunity to enrich the answer.
    The user will provide a question, and you will scan through the provided
     information to see if the question is answered.
    If anything is missing from the answer, you will provide a set of new
     questions that can be asked to gather the missing information.
    All new questions must be complete, atomic, and specific.
    However, if the provided information is enough to answer the original
     question, you will respond with an empty list.

    JSON template to use for finding missing information:
    {
        "questions": ["question1", "question2"]
    }
"""
```

We follow the same pattern as before with the JSON format and the instructions to the LLM.

Next, we'll have a look at the function that calls the LLM.

Listing 5.11 Answer critic function

```
def critique_answers(question: str, answers: list[dict[str, str]]) -> list[str]:
    messages = [
        {
            "role": "system",
            "content": answer_critique_prompt,
        },
        *answers,
        {
            "role": "user",
            "content": f"The original user question to answer: {question}",
        },
    ]
    config = {"response_format": {"type": "json_object"}}
    output = chat(messages, model="gpt-4o", config=config)
    try:
        return json.loads(output)["questions"]
    except json.JSONDecodeError:
        print("Error decoding JSON")
    return []
```

This function takes the original question and the answers from the retrievers and calls the LLM to check if the original question is answered correctly. If the question is not answered correctly, the LLM will return a list of new questions that can be asked to gather the missing information.

If we get a list of new questions back, we can go through the retriever router again to get the missing information. We should also have some exit criteria from this loop so we don't get stuck in a loop where we can't get the answer to the original question from the retrievers.

5.3.4 Tying it all together

So far, we have implemented the retriever agents, the retriever router, and the answer critic. The final piece is to tie it all together in a main function that takes in the user input and returns the answer to the user, if the answer is available.

The following listing shows what the main function might look like. Let's start with the instructions to the LLM.

Listing 5.12 Agentic RAG main instructions

```
main_prompt = """
    Your job is to help the user with their questions.
    You will receive user questions and information needed to answer the
     questions
    If the information is missing to answer part of or the whole question,
     you will say that the information
    is missing. You will only use the information provided to you in the
     prompt to answer the questions.
    You are not allowed to make anything up or use external information.
"""
```

It's very important that the LLM only uses the information provided to it in the prompt to answer the questions. This is to make sure that the system is consistent and that we can trust the answers it provides.

Next, we'll have a look at the main function.

Listing 5.13 Agentic RAG main function

```
def main(input: str):
    answers = handle_user_input(input)
    critique = critique_answers(input, answers)

    if critique:
        answers = handle_user_input(" ".join(critique), answers)

    llm_response = chat(
        [
            {"role": "system", "content": main_prompt},
            *answers,
            {"role": "user", "content": f"The user question to answer: {input}"},
        ],
        model="gpt-4o",
    )

    return llm_response
```

The main function runs the user input through the agentic RAG system and returns the answer to the user. If the answer is not complete or is incorrect, the critique function will return a list of new questions that can be asked to gather the missing information.

We only critique the answers once; if the answers are still incomplete or incorrect after the critique, we return the answers to the user as is and rely on the LLM to let the user know what's incomplete.

Summary

- Agentic RAG is a system where a variety of retrieval agents are available to retrieve the data needed to answer the user question.
- The main interface to an agentic RAG system is usually some kind of use case or retriever router, whose job is to find the best-suited retriever (or retrievers) to perform the task at hand.
- The foundational parts of an agentic RAG system are retriever agents, retriever router, and answer critic.
- The main parts of an agentic RAG system can be implemented using an LLM with tools/function-calling support.
- The retriever agents can be generic or specialized and should be added over time as needed to improve the performance of the application.
- The answer critic is a function that takes in the answers from the retrievers and checks if the original question is answered correctly.

6 Constructing knowledge graphs with LLMs

This chapter covers

- Structured data extraction
- Different approaches to extraction

In this chapter, you will explore the process of constructing knowledge graphs using LLMs from unstructured sources like text documents. The focus will be on how LLMs can extract and structure data from raw text, transforming it into usable formats for building knowledge graphs.

In previous chapters, you learned about basic techniques for document chunking, embedding, and retrieval (chapter 2), as well as more advanced methods for improving retrieval accuracy (chapter 3). However, as you learned in chapter 4, relying solely on text embeddings can lead to challenges in scenarios where data needs to be structured to answer questions that require filtering, counting, or aggregation operations. To solve the limitations of only using text embeddings, you will learn how to transform unstructured data into structured formats suitable for knowledge graph construction, using LLMs for automated data extraction. By the end of the chapter, you will be able to extract structured information from raw text, design a knowledge graph model for the extracted data, and import this data into a graph database.

You'll begin by exploring a common challenge in legal document retrieval—managing multiple contracts and their terms—and learn how structured data extraction provides a solution. Throughout the chapter, you'll follow examples that illustrate the process and guide you step by step through the workflow of constructing a knowledge graph from unstructured text.

6.1 Extracting structured data from text

Much of the information found online, and even within companies, exists in unstructured formats like various documents. However, there are situations where the simple retrieval technique using only text embeddings falls short. Legal documents are one such example.

For instance, if you're asking about the payment terms in a contract with ACME Inc., it's crucial to ensure that the terms are actually from that specific contract and not from others. When you simply chunk and retrieve across multiple legal documents, the top `k` chunks you get at retrieval could come from different, unrelated documents, causing confusion, as shown in figure 6.1.

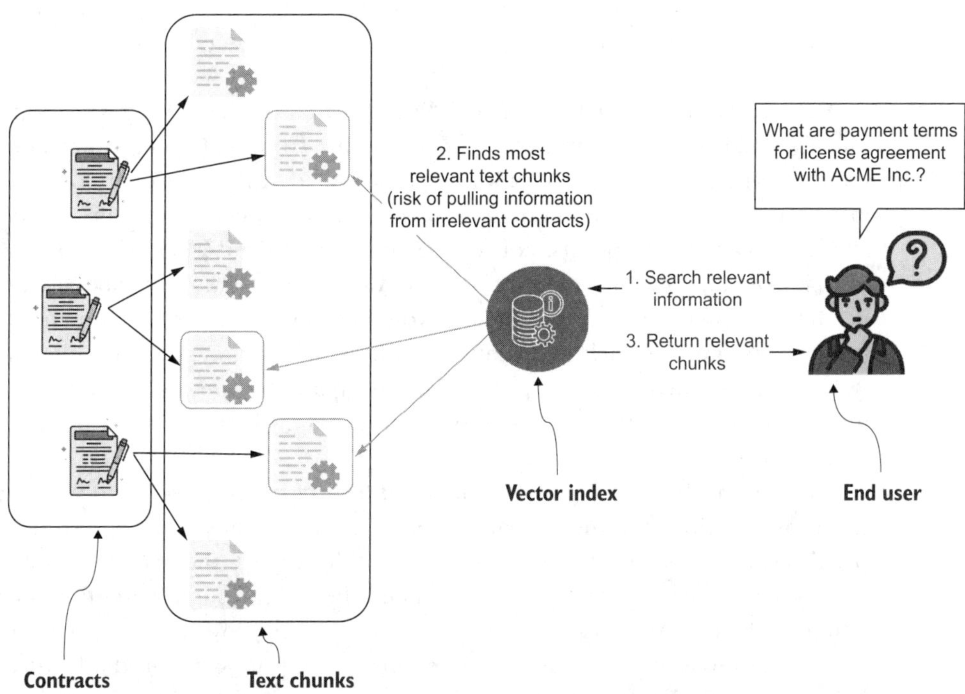

Figure 6.1 Basic vector retrieval strategy might return chunks from various contracts.

Figure 6.1 illustrates how contract documents are broken down into text chunks and indexed using text embeddings. When an end user asks a specific question, such as about the payment terms of a particular contract, the system retrieves the most relevant chunks. However, if multiple contracts contain different payment terms, the retrieval process may unintentionally pull information from various documents, mixing relevant chunks from the target contract with irrelevant ones from others. This happens because the system focuses on retrieving top-ranked text chunks based on similarity, without always distinguishing whether the chunks come from the correct contract. As a result, chunks that share keywords like "payment" or "terms" but belong to different contracts may be included, leading to a fragmented and inconsistent view of the terms. This confusion can then be responsible when the LLM tries to synthesize these mixed chunks into a coherent answer, ultimately increasing the risk of inaccurate or misleading information.

Additionally, consider the following question: How many active contracts do we currently have with ACME Inc.? To answer this, you would first need to filter all contracts based on their active status and then count the relevant ones. These types of queries resemble traditional business intelligence questions, where the text-embedding approach falls short.

Text embeddings are primarily designed to retrieve semantically similar content, not to handle operations like filtering, sorting, or aggregating data. To handle such operations, structured data is required, as text embeddings alone are not well-suited for these operations.

For some domains, structuring data is vital when implementing RAG applications. Luckily, LLMs excel at extracting structured data from text due to their deep understanding of natural language, allowing them to identify relevant information accurately. They can be finetuned or guided through specific prompts to locate and extract required data points, converting unstructured information into a structured format like tables or key–value pairs. Using LLMs for structured data extraction is particularly useful when dealing with large volumes of documents where manually identifying and organizing such information would be labor intensive and time consuming. By automating the extraction process, LLMs enable businesses to transform unstructured information into actionable, structured data, which can then be used for further analysis or RAG applications.

Imagine you're working at a company as a software engineer, and you're part of a team tasked with building a chatbot that can answer questions based on the company's legal documents. Since this is a large-scale project, the team is divided into two groups: one focused on data preparation and the other on implementing the retrieval systems described in chapters 4 and 5. You're assigned to the data preparation team, where your job is to process legal documents and extract structured information. This information will be used to build a knowledge graph, following the workflow visualized in figure 6.2.

The workflow visualized in figure 6.2 begins with contract documents as input, which are processed using an LLM to extract structured information. In the legal domain, you can extract various details such as involved parties, dates, terms, and

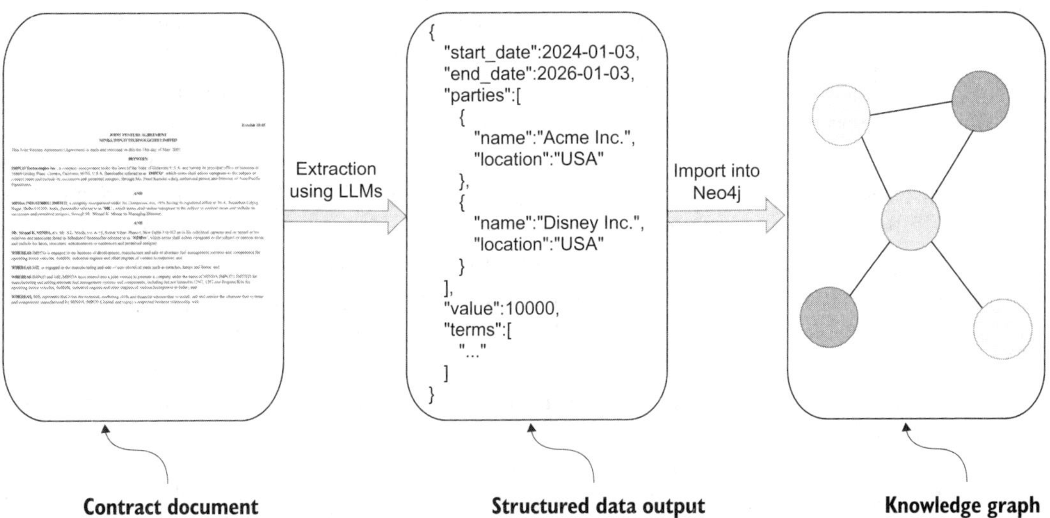

Figure 6.2 Building knowledge graphs from text by using LLMs to extract structured data information

more. Here, the structured output is represented in a JSON format, and this structured information is then stored in Neo4j, which will serve as the foundation for the legal chatbot's data retrieval.

These two examples highlight the limitations of simple text embeddings when it comes to handling specific, structured queries, such as asking for payment terms in a contract or counting active agreements. In both cases, accurate answers require structured data rather than relying solely on the semantic similarity of unstructured text. In the remainder of this chapter, we'll dive deeper into how LLMs can be effectively used to extract structured data from complex documents and how this structured output plays a critical role in constructing reliable knowledge graphs for advanced retrieval tasks. To follow along, you'll need access to a running, blank Neo4j instance. This can be a local installation or a cloud-hosted instance; just make sure it's empty. You can follow the implementation directly in the accompanying Jupyter notebook available here: https://github.com/tomasonjo/kg-rag/blob/main/notebooks/ch06.ipynb.

Let's dive in.

6.1.1 *Structured Outputs model definition*

Extracting structured data from text is not a new idea; it has been a vital task in data processing for many years. Historically, this process was known as *information extraction* and required complex systems, often relying on multiple machine learning models working together. These systems were typically expensive to build and maintain, requiring a team of skilled engineers and domain experts to ensure they functioned correctly. Due to these reasons, only large organizations with substantial resources could afford to implement such solutions. The high cost and technical barriers made it inaccessible for many businesses and individuals. However, advancements in LLMs have dramatically simplified the process. Today, users can prompt an LLM to extract structured information with a much lower technical threshold instead of building and training multiple models. This shift has opened up a wide range of use cases for structured data extraction.

Extracting structured data using LLMs has become such a common use case that OpenAI introduced a Structured Outputs feature in its API to simplify and standardize the process. This feature allows developers to define the expected output format ahead of time, ensuring that the model's response adheres to a specific structure. Structured Outputs is not a separate library; it is a built-in capability of the OpenAI API, available through function calling or schema definitions. For example, in Python, developers often use libraries like Pydantic to define data schemas. These schemas can then be passed to the model, guiding it to produce outputs that match the specified format, as shown in the following listing.

Listing 6.1 Defining the desired output using the Pydantic library

```
from pydantic import BaseModel

class CalendarEvent(BaseModel):
    name: str
    date: str = Field(..., description="The date of the event. Use yyyy-MM-dd
     format")
    participants: list[str]
```

The `CalendarEvent` class in listing 6.1 represents a structured way to capture details about an event. It includes a name for the event, a date when it will occur, and a list of participants. By defining these attributes explicitly, it ensures that any event data conforms to this structure, making it easier to extract and work with event information in a reliable and consistent manner. The available types for attributes are

- String
- Number
- Boolean
- Integer
- Object
- Array
- Enum
- anyOf

Let's examine the definition of the `date` attribute.

Listing 6.2 `date` attribute

```
date: str = Field(..., description="The date of the event. Use yyyy-MM-dd format")
```

The code in listing 6.2 provides instructions on how to extract data for the `date` attribute. Naming the attribute `date` signals to the model to focus on date-related information.

By using the `str` type, we specify that the extracted information should be represented as a string, as there's no native datetime type available. Additionally, the `description` clarifies the desired `yyyy-MM-dd` format. This step is crucial because, although the model knows it's dealing with a string, the description ensures that the date follows the specific format. Without this guidance, the `str` type alone might not convey enough detail about the expected output structure.

Structured Outputs significantly simplifies the development process by ensuring that the LLM responses adhere to a predefined schema. This reduces the need for post-processing and validation, allowing developers to focus on using the data within their systems. The feature provides type safety, guaranteeing that responses are always correctly formatted, and eliminates the need for complex prompts to achieve consistent output, making the process more efficient and reliable overall.

The first step in extracting structured output from legal documents is to define the contract data model that needs to be extracted. Since you're a software engineer and not a legal expert, it's important to consult someone with domain knowledge to determine which information is most important to extract. Additionally, speaking with end users about the specific questions they want answered can provide valuable insights.

Following these initial discussions, you propose the contract data model shown in the following listing.

Listing 6.3 Defining the desired output using a Pydantic object

```
class Contract(BaseModel):
    """
    Represents the key details of the contract.
    """

    contract_type: str = Field(
        ...,
        description="The type of contract being entered into.",
        enum=contract_types,
    )
    parties: List[Organization] = Field(
        ...,
        description="List of parties involved in the contract, with details
 of each party's role.",
    )
    effective_date: str = Field(
        ...,
        description="The date when the contract becomes effective. Use yyyy-
 MM-dd format.",
    )
    term: str = Field(
        ...,
        description="The duration of the agreement, including provisions for
 renewal or termination.",
    )
    contract_scope: str = Field(
        ...,
```

Description of the extracted object

Using enum to define the possible values an LLM can use

An attribute can be an object like the Organization in this example.

Since the datetime type isn't available, you want to define the date format to be extracted.

```
        description="Description of the scope of the contract, including
     rights, duties, and any limitations.",
    )
    end_date: Optional[str] = Field(        <-- You can use Optional for attributes
        ...,                                    that might not appear in all contracts.
        description="The date when the contract becomes expires. Use yyyy-MM-
      dd format.",
    )
    total_amount: Optional[float] = Field(
        ..., description="Total value of the contract."
    )
    governing_law: Optional[Location] = Field(
        ..., description="The jurisdiction's laws governing the contract."
    )
```

The class name, `Contract`, along with the concise docstring, "Represents the key details of the contract," provide the LLM with a high-level understanding that the desired output should capture essential contractual information. This guides the model to focus on extracting and organizing key details, such as the contract type, involved parties, dates, and financials.

In general, attributes can be categorized as either mandatory or optional. When an attribute is optional, you designate it with an `Optional` type, indicating to the LLM that the information may or may not be present. It's vital to mark attributes as optional when information could be missing, as otherwise, some LLMs may hallucinate values in an attempt to fill the gaps. For instance, `total_amount` is optional since some contracts are simply agreements with no monetary exchange. Conversely, the `effective_date` attribute is mandatory, as you expect each contract to have a starting date.

Notice how each attribute includes a `description` value to provide clear guidance to the LLM, ensuring it extracts the desired information accurately. This is a good practice, even when some attributes seem obvious. In some cases, you may also want to specify the allowed values for a particular attribute. You can achieve this by using the `enum` parameter. For example, the `contract_type` attribute utilizes the `enum` parameter to inform the LLM of the specific categories to apply. The following listing contains the available values for the `contract_type` parameter.

Listing 6.4 Contract type enum values

```
contract_types = [
    "Service Agreement",
    "Licensing Agreement",
    "Non-Disclosure Agreement (NDA)",
    "Partnership Agreement",
    "Lease Agreement"
]
```

Clearly, the list in listing 6.4 is not exhaustive, as there are additional options that could be included.

Some attributes may be more complex and can be defined as custom objects. For instance, the `parties` attribute is a list of `Organization` objects. A list is used because contracts typically involve multiple parties, and a custom object allows for extracting more than just a simple string about a specific attribute. The code in the following listing defines the `Organization` object.

Listing 6.5 Custom `Organization` object

```
class Organization(BaseModel):
    """
    Represents an organization, including its name and location.
    """

    name: str = Field(..., description="The name of the organization.")
    location: Location = Field(
        ..., description="The primary location of the organization."
    )
    role: str = Field(
        ...,
        description="The role of the organization in the contract, such as
➥ 'provider', 'client', 'supplier', etc.",
    )
```

You can provide possible values in the description instead of enum if you aren't providing all possible values but only examples.

The `Organization` object in listing 6.5 captures the key details of an organization involved in the contract, including its name, primary location, and role. The `location` attribute is a nested `Location` object, allowing us to structure the information into values like city, state, and country. As you can see, we can have nested objects, but the typical advice is to avoid too many levels of nested objects for better performance. For the `role` attribute, we've provided examples like "provider" and "client" but opted not to use an enum to avoid restricting the values. This flexibility is important, as the exact roles may vary and aren't entirely predictable. By defining the organization this way, the LLM is guided to extract more detailed and structured information about the parties involved.

Lastly, you need to define the `Location` object.

Listing 6.6 Custom `Location` object

```
class Location(BaseModel):
    """
    Represents a physical location including address, city, state, and country.
    """

    address: Optional[str] = Field(
        ..., description="The street address of the location."
    )
    city: Optional[str] = Field(..., description="The city of the location.")
```

```
    state: Optional[str] = Field(
        ..., description="The state or region of the location."
    )
    country: str = Field(
        ...,
        description="The country of the location. Use the two-letter ISO
     standard.",
    )
```

LLMs are familiar with ISO standards being used for countries, so you instruct the model to standardize values based on a specific standard.

The `Location` object represents a physical address, capturing details such as the street address, city, state or region, and country. All attributes, except for the `country`, are optional, allowing flexibility when full location details may not be available. For the `country` attribute, we guide the LLM to use the two-letter ISO standard, ensuring consistency and making it easier to work with and process across different systems. This structure enables the LLM to extract standardized, usable information while allowing for incomplete or partial data when necessary.

You've now defined the contract data model, which can be used to extract relevant information from the company's contracts. This model will serve as the blueprint for guiding LLMs in structured data extraction. With a clear understanding of the data structure in place, it's time to explore how you can effectively prompt the LLM to extract this information.

6.1.2 Structured Outputs extraction request

With the contract data model defined, you now have a data definition that LLMs can follow to extract structured information. The next step is to ensure that the LLM understands exactly how to output this data in a consistent format. This is where OpenAI's Structured Outputs feature comes in. By using this feature, you can guide the LLM's behavior to output data that strictly adheres to the contract model while using the same chat template introduced in previous chapters.

The Structured Outputs documentation (https://mng.bz/oZZp) uses system messages to additionally guide the LLM to focus on the task at hand. By using a system message, as shown in the following listing, you can provide clear instructions to steer the model's behavior effectively.

Listing 6.7 System message for structured output extraction

```
system_message = """
You are an expert in extracting structured information from legal documents
     and contracts.
Identify key details such as parties involved, dates, terms, obligations, and
     legal definitions.
Present the extracted information in a clear, structured format. Be concise,
     focusing on essential
legal content and ignoring unnecessary boilerplate language. The extracted
     data will be used to address
any questions that may arise regarding the contracts."""
```

It's difficult to provide precise instructions for crafting the ideal system message. What's clear is that you should define the domain and provide the LLM with context on how the output will be used. Beyond that, it often comes down to trial and error.

Finally, you define a function that takes any text as input and outputs a dictionary as defined by the contract data model.

Listing 6.8 System message for structured output extraction

```
def extract(document, model="gpt-4o-2024-08-06", temperature=0):
    response = client.beta.chat.completions.parse(
        model=model,
        temperature=temperature,
        messages=[
            {"role": "system", "content": system_message},
            {"role": "user", "content": document},
        ],
        response_format=Contract,
    )
    return json.loads(response.choices[0].message.content)
```

Passing in system message as first message

The document is passed as a user message without any additional instructions.

The output format is defined using the response_format parameters.

The extract function in listing 6.8 processes a text document and returns a dictionary based on the contract data model. It utilizes the latest GPT-4o model available at the time of writing, which supports structured output. The function sends a system message to guide the LLM, followed by the raw user-provided document text without any modifications. The response is then formatted according to the `Contract` data model and returned as a dictionary.

To see this process in action, let's now look at how we can apply this method using a real-world dataset. Since accessing proprietary contracts can be difficult due to confidentiality, you will use a public dataset titled the Contract Understanding Atticus Dataset (CUAD).

6.1.3 CUAD dataset

While all companies have contracts and legal documents, these are typically not public due to the sensitive nature of the information they contain. For the purpose of this demonstration, we will use a single text document from the CUAD dataset (Hendrycks et al., 2021). CUAD is a specialized corpus created for training AI models to understand and review legal contracts.

The following listing shows an improved version. The contract is available in the accompanying GitHub repository of the book, eliminating the need to download the entire dataset. The code handles opening the file and reading its content.

Listing 6.9 Reading the contract text document

```
with open('../data/license_agreement.txt', 'r') as file:
    contents = file.read()
```

Reads the file

You can now process the contract by executing the code shown in the following listing.

Listing 6.10 Extracting structured information from text

```
data = extract(contents)
print(data)
```

The results will look similar to the following listing.

Listing 6.11 Results of the extraction

```
{'contract_type': 'Licensing Agreement',
 'parties': [{'name': 'Mortgage Logic.com, Inc.',
   'location': {'address': 'Two Venture Plaza, 2 Venture',
    'city': 'Irvine',
    'state': 'California',
    'country': 'US'},
   'role': 'Client'},
  {'name': 'TrueLink, Inc.',
   'location': {'address': '3026 South Higuera',
    'city': 'San Luis Obispo',
    'state': 'California',
    'country': 'US'},
   'role': 'Provider'}],
 'effective_date': '1999-02-26',
 'term': "1 year, with automatic renewal for successive one-year periods
     unless terminated with 30 days' notice prior to the end of the term.",
 'contract_scope': 'TrueLink grants Mortgage Logic.com a nonexclusive license
     to use the Interface for origination, underwriting, processing, and
     funding of consumer finance receivables. TrueLink will provide hosting
     services, including storage, response time management, bandwidth,
     availability, access to usage statistics, backups, internet connection,
     and domain name assistance. TrueLink will also provide support services
     and transmit credit data as permitted under applicable agreements and
     laws.',
 'end_date': None,
 'total_amount': None,
 'governing_law': {'address': None,
  'city': None,
  'state': 'California',
  'country': 'US'}}
```

The extracted contract data is organized into structured fields, though not all attributes are fully populated. For instance, some fields like `end_date` and `total_amount` are marked as `None`, indicating missing or unspecified information. Meanwhile, attributes such as the `contract_scope` contain more detailed, descriptive text that outlines the operational details of the agreement, such as the services provided and responsibilities. The structure includes a clear breakdown of the parties involved, their roles, and locations. The contract also specifies its start date and renewal conditions, but other financial or termination details remain undefined as they are missing in the contract.

Exercise 6.1

Download the CUAD dataset and explore creating various contract data models based on different types of contracts. Once you've defined different models, you can test and refine them by analyzing how well they capture and categorize the key legal information across the contracts.

In this section, you successfully extracted structured data from a contract document using the CUAD dataset and the contract data model defined earlier. The LLM was guided to identify key contract details, and the results were formatted in a structured way, allowing you to organize important information such as contract type, parties, and terms. This process demonstrates how LLMs can efficiently transform unstructured legal documents into actionable data.

Now that you've seen how to extract structured information from legal contracts, the next section will focus on how to incorporate this data into a knowledge graph.

6.2 Constructing the graph

As the final step in the chapter, you'll import the extracted structured output into Neo4j. This follows the standard approach for importing structured data. First, you should design a suitable graph model that represents the relationships and entities in your data. Graph modeling is beyond the scope of this book, but you can use LLMs to assist in defining the graph schema or look at other learning material such as Neo4j Graph Academy.

An example of a contract graph model is illustrated in figure 6.3, which you will be using in this step. The graph model represents a contract system with three main entities: `Contract`, `Organization`, and `Location`. The `Contract` node stores details such as its ID, type, effective date, term, total amount, governing law, and scope.

Organizations are linked to contracts through the `HAS_PARTY` relationship, and each organization has a `HAS_LOCATION` relationship to a `Location` node, which captures the organization's address, city, state, and country. Locations are represented as separate nodes to accommodate the possibility that a single organization may have multiple addresses.

Now that you've defined the graph model, the next step is to begin the process of constructing the knowledge graph. This involves several key steps, each of which will be covered in the following subsections. First, you'll define unique constraints and indexes to ensure data integrity and improve performance. After that, you'll import the structured contract data into Neo4j using a Cypher statement. Once the data is loaded, you will visualize the graph to confirm that all entities and relationships are correctly represented. Finally, we'll address important data refinement tasks, such as entity resolution, which ensures that different representations of the same real-world entity are merged correctly, and we'll touch on how to handle both structured and unstructured data in the graph.

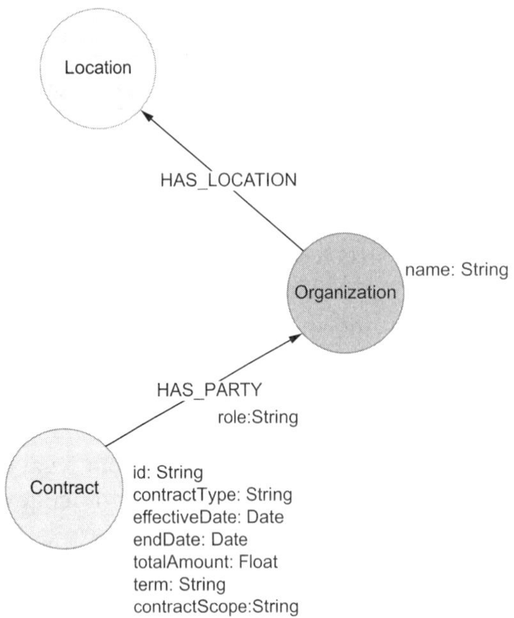

Figure 6.3 Contract graph model

6.2.1 Data import

Defining unique constraints and indexes wherever applicable is a best practice, as it not only ensures the integrity of the graph but also enhances query performance. The code in the following listing defines unique constraints for `Contract`, `Organization`, and `Location` nodes.

Listing 6.12 Defining the unique constraints

```
neo4j_driver.execute_query(
    "CREATE CONSTRAINT IF NOT EXISTS FOR (c:Contract) REQUIRE c.id IS UNIQUE;"
)
neo4j_driver.execute_query(
    "CREATE CONSTRAINT IF NOT EXISTS FOR (o:Organization) REQUIRE o.name IS
     UNIQUE;"
)
neo4j_driver.execute_query(
    "CREATE CONSTRAINT IF NOT EXISTS FOR (l:Location) REQUIRE l.fullAddress IS
     UNIQUE;"
)
```

Next, you need to prepare an import Cypher statement that will take the dictionary output and load it into Neo4j, adhering to the graph schema outlined in figure 6.3. The import Cypher statement is shown in the following listing.

Listing 6.13 Defining the import Cypher statement

```
import_query = """WITH $data AS contract_data
MERGE (contract:Contract {id: randomUUID()})          <-- Creates the Contract node
SET contract += {                                          using a random UUID as
  contract_type: contract_data.contract_type,              unique identifier
  effective_date: contract_data.effective_date,
  term: contract_data.term,
  contract_scope: contract_data.contract_scope,
  end_date: contract_data.end_date,
  total_amount: contract_data.total_amount,
  governing_law: contract_data.governing_law.state + ' ' +
                 contract_data.governing_law.country
}
WITH contract, contract_data
UNWIND contract_data.parties AS party              <-- Creates the Party
MERGE (p:Organization {name: party.name})              nodes and their
MERGE (loc:Location {                                  locations
  fullAddress: party.location.address + ' ' +
               party.location.city + ' ' +
               party.location.state + ' ' +
               party.location.country})
SET loc += {
  address: party.location.address,
  city: party.location.city,
  state: party.location.state,
  country: party.location.country
}                                                  Links parties to
MERGE (p)-[:LOCATED_AT]->(loc)                 <-- their location
MERGE (p)-[r:HAS_PARTY]->(contract)             <-- Links parties to
SET r.role = party.role                             the contract
"""
```

Explaining Cypher statements, such as the one in listing 6.13, is outside the scope of this book. However, if you need assistance, LLMs can help clarify the details and provide a deeper understanding of the Cypher statement. However, we want to highlight that the query in listing 6.13 is not idempotent due to the use of `randomUUID()` for the contract ID. As a result, running the query multiple times will create duplicate contract entries in the database, each with a unique ID.

Now that everything is prepared, you can execute the code in the following listing to import the contract into Neo4j.

Listing 6.14 Importing the contract data into Neo4j

```
neo4j_driver.execute_query(import_query, data=data)
```

Once the import is successful, you can open the Neo4j browser to explore the generated graph, which should closely resemble the visualization shown in figure 6.4.

The visualization in figure 6.4 depicts a graph where a central "Licensing Agreement" (representing a contract) is linked to two organizations: "Mortgage Logic.com,

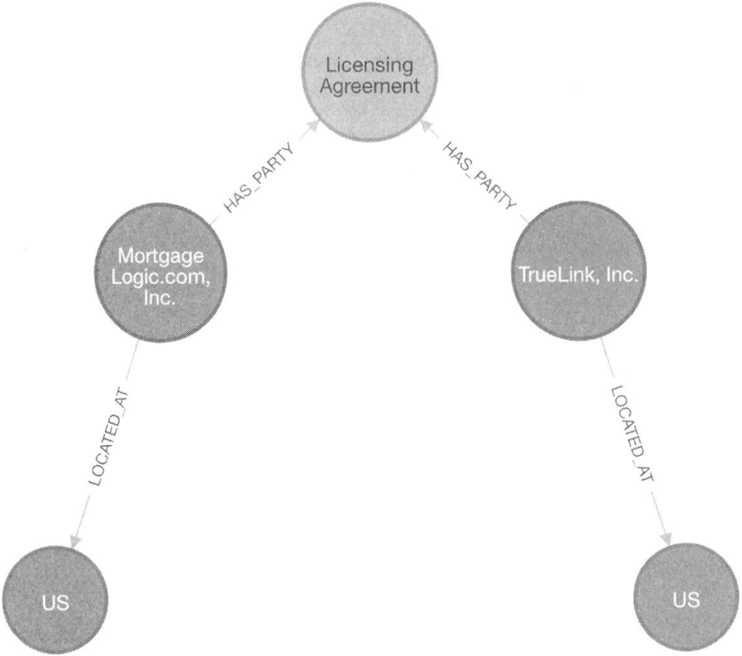

Figure 6.4 Contract graph data visualized

Inc." and "TrueLink, Inc." via the relationship HAS_PARTY. Each organization is further connected to a "US" node representing their location through the LOCATED_AT relationship.

6.2.2 Entity resolution

You've successfully imported the graph, but your work isn't done yet. In most cases, especially when dealing with natural language processing or LLM-driven data processing, some level of data cleaning is necessary. One of the most crucial steps in this cleaning process is entity resolution. Entity resolution refers to the process of identifying and merging different representations of the same real-world entity within a dataset or knowledge graph. When working with large and diverse datasets, it's common for the same entity to appear in multiple forms due to inconsistencies like spelling variations, different naming conventions, or even slight discrepancies in data formats, as shown in figure 6.5, where we see three nodes representing variations of the same entity. The three names are

- UTI Asset Management Company
- UTI Asset Management Company Limited
- UTI Asset Management Company Ltd

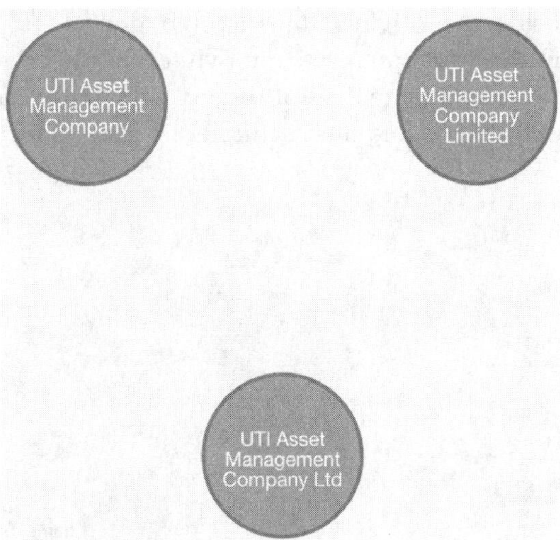

Figure 6.5 Potential duplicates

Entity resolution in this context involves identifying that all these variations refer to the same real-world organization, despite minor differences in naming conventions (such as "Limited" vs. "Ltd"). The goal of entity resolution is to unify these disparate references into a single, coherent node within the graph. This not only improves data integrity but also enhances the graph's ability to make more accurate inferences and relationships. Techniques used in entity resolution include string matching, clustering algorithms, and even machine learning methods that use the context surrounding each entity to detect and resolve duplicates.

It is important to note that entity resolution is highly use case and domain specific. A generic, one-size-fits-all solution rarely works because each domain has its own naming conventions, data schemas, and nuances in how entities are represented. For instance, the methods and thresholds that might work well for resolving organizations in a financial dataset could produce suboptimal results when dealing with biological entities in a healthcare setting. Consequently, one of the most effective strategies is to develop domain-specific ontologies or rules that reflect your particular data context. Additionally, using subject matter experts to define matching criteria and using iterative feedback loops—where potential matches are verified or corrected—can greatly improve accuracy. By combining domain expertise with context-aware machine learning or clustering techniques, you can develop a more robust and flexible approach to entity resolution. This will ensure that you capture the subtle details that matter most in your unique data environment.

6.2.3 Adding unstructured data to the graph

Knowledge graphs are increasingly used to store both structured and unstructured data, a scenario that has become even more common with the advent of LLMs. In this context, LLMs can be used to extract structured data from unstructured sources like text documents. However, storing the original unstructured documents and the extracted structured data within the graph preserves the richness of the original data while enabling more precise querying and analysis of the extracted information. An expanded graph schema where structured and unstructured information is combined is presented in figure 6.6.

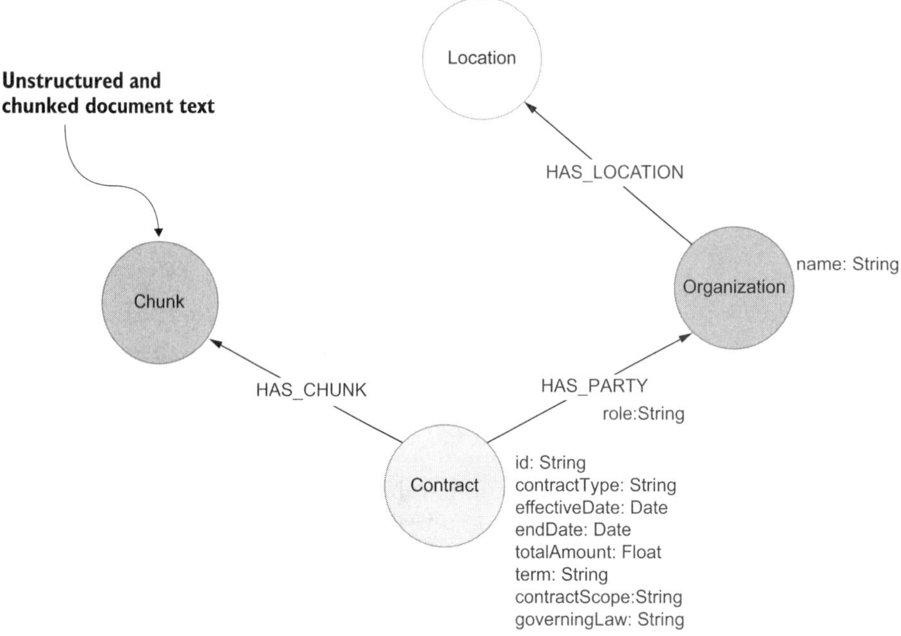

Figure 6.6 Expanded graph model with added unstructured data

When incorporating unstructured data into a graph, it's common to use a simple chunking strategy based on token count or word length to split text into manageable segments. While this naive approach works for general use cases, certain domains, such as legal contracts, benefit from more specialized chunking methods. For example, splitting a contract by its clauses preserves its semantic structure and improves the quality of downstream analysis. This smarter approach allows the graph to capture more meaningful relationships, enabling richer insights and more accurate inferences.

This chapter has guided you through constructing knowledge graphs from unstructured data using LLMs. You explored the limitations of text embeddings in handling structured queries and learned how structured data extraction provides a solution. By defining data models, prompting LLMs for extraction, and importing the results into a graph database, you saw how to transform raw text into usable data for knowledge graphs. Additionally, we covered key tasks like entity resolution and combining structured and unstructured data for richer insights. With this knowledge, you can now apply structured data extraction in practical scenarios.

Summary

- Simply chunking documents for retrieval can result in inaccurate or mixed results, especially in domains like legal documents where document boundaries matter.
- Retrieval tasks like filtering, sorting, and aggregating require structured data, as text embeddings alone are not suited for such operations.
- LLMs are effective at extracting structured data from unstructured text, converting it into usable formats like tables or key–value pairs.
- Structured output features in LLMs allow developers to define schemas, ensuring responses follow a specific format and reducing the need for postprocessing.
- Defining a clear data model with attributes such as contract type, parties, and dates is essential for guiding LLMs to extract relevant information accurately.
- Entity resolution in knowledge graphs is important for merging different representations of the same entity, improving data consistency and accuracy.
- Combining structured and unstructured data in knowledge graphs preserves the richness of the source material while enabling more precise querying.

7 Microsoft's GraphRAG implementation

This chapter covers

- Introducing Microsoft's GraphRAG
- Extracting and summarizing entities and relationships
- Calculating and summarizing communities of entities
- Implementing global and local search techniques

In chapter 6, you learned how to extract structured information from legal documents to build a knowledge graph. In this chapter, you will explore a slightly different extraction and processing pipeline using Microsoft's GraphRAG (Edge et al., 2024) approach. This end-to-end example still constructs a knowledge graph but places greater emphasis on natural language summarization of entities and their relationships. The whole pipeline is visualized in figure 7.1.

A key innovation of Microsoft's GraphRAG (MS GraphRAG: https://github.com/microsoft/graphrag) is its use of an LLM to build a knowledge graph through a two-stage process. In the first stage, entities and relationships are extracted and summarized from source documents to form the foundation of the knowledge graph, as illustrated in the steps up to the Knowledge Graph in figure 7.1. What distinguishes MS GraphRAG is that, once the knowledge graph has been constructed,

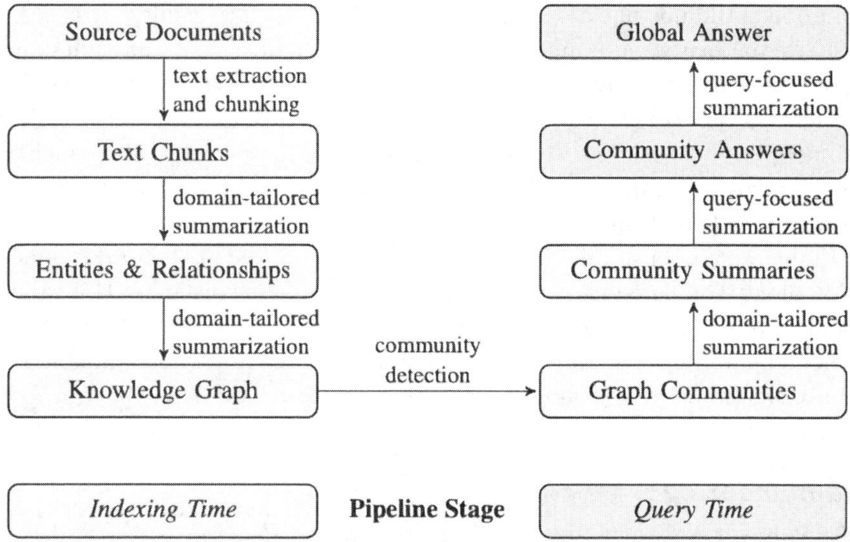

Figure 7.1 Microsoft's GraphRAG pipeline. (Image from Edge et al., 2024, licensed under CC BY 4.0)

graph communities are detected, and domain-specific summaries are generated for groups of closely related entities. This layered approach transforms fragmented pieces of information from various text chunks into a cohesive and organized representation of information about specified entities, relationships, and communities.

These entity- and community-level summaries can then be used to provide relevant information in response to user queries in a RAG application. With such a structured knowledge graph, multiple retrieval approaches can be applied. In this chapter, you'll explore both global and local search retrieval approaches described in the MS GraphRAG paper.

7.1 Dataset selection

MS GraphRAG is designed to process unstructured text documents by extracting key entities and generating summaries that connect information across multiple text chunks. To ensure meaningful insights, our dataset should not only be rich in entity information but also contain entity data spread across multiple chunks. Since entity types are a configurable aspect of MS GraphRAG, they must be defined in advance. Relevant entities typically include people, organizations, and locations but can also extend to domain-specific concepts such as genes and pathways in medicine or legal clauses in law.

To make an informed decision about the entity types, it is important to explore the dataset and identify the types of questions you want to answer. The choice of entity types shapes the entire downstream process, influencing extraction, linking, and summarization quality.

For example, the MS GraphRAG paper utilized datasets from podcasts and news articles. In both cases, entities such as people, organizations, and locations are commonly mentioned. Additionally, depending on the subject, such as gaming or healthy lifestyle podcasts, you may want to include domain-specific entities, like game titles, health conditions, or nutritional concepts, to ensure comprehensive extraction and analysis.

Here we use *The Odyssey* to evaluate MS GraphRAG, as it features a rich narrative with people, gods, mystical weapons, and more. Moreover, key entities such as Ulysses appear across multiple text chunks, making it a suitable dataset for testing entity extraction and cross-chunk summarizations.

In the remainder of this chapter, you'll implement the MS GraphRAG method. To follow along, you'll need access to a running, blank Neo4j instance. This can be a local installation or a cloud-hosted instance; just make sure it's empty. You can follow the implementation directly in the accompanying Jupyter notebook available at https://github.com/tomasonjo/kg-rag/blob/main/notebooks/ch07.ipynb.

Let's dive in.

7.2 Graph indexing

Here you will construct the knowledge graph and generate entity and community summaries. Throughout this construction, you'll explore key considerations at each step, including entity selection, graph connectivity, and how these choices influence the quality of summaries and queries.

Start by loading *The Odyssey* from the Gutenberg project (https://www.gutenberg.org/ebooks/1727).

Listing 7.1 Loading *The Odyssey*

```
url = "https://www.gutenberg.org/cache/epub/1727/pg1727.txt"
response = requests.get(url)
```

With the text prepared, you can now walk through the MS GraphRAG pipeline.

7.2.1 Chunking

The Odyssey consists of 24 books of varying lengths. Your first task is to remove prefaces and footnotes and then divide the text into individual books, as demonstrated in the following listing. This approach follows the narrative's natural divisions, providing a semantically meaningful way to structure the text.

Listing 7.2 Removing preface and footnotes and splitting into books

```
def chunk_into_books(text: str) -> List[str]:
    return (
        text.split("PREFACE TO FIRST EDITION")[2]
        .split("FOOTNOTES")[0]
        .strip()
        .split("\nBOOK")[1:]
    )

books = chunk_into_books(response.text)
```

Now you need to check the number of tokens in each book to determine whether further chunking is necessary. The code in the following listing provides basic statistics on the token counts of the books.

Listing 7.3 Counting the number of tokens in books

```
token_count = [num_tokens_from_string(el) for el in books]
print(
    f"""There are {len(token_count)} books with token sizes:
- avg {sum(token_count) / len(token_count)}
- min {min(token_count)}
- max {max(token_count)}
"""
)
```

The token counts across the 24 books vary significantly, with an average of 6,515 tokens, a minimum of 4,459, and a maximum of 10,760. Given this range, further chunking is necessary to ensure that no individual section exceeds reasonable token limits.

But what are reasonable chunk sizes? The researchers behind MS GraphRAG compared different chunk sizes and analyzed their effect on the overall number of extracted entities. The results of this comparison are shown in figure 7.2.

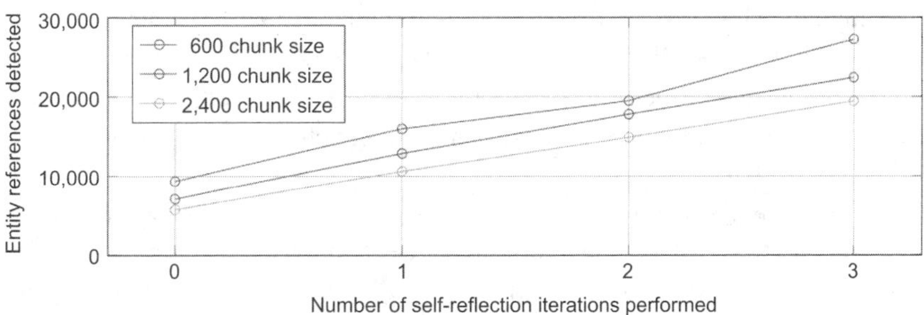

Figure 7.2 Impact of chunk size and self-reflection iterations on entity extraction. (Image from Edge et al., 2024, licensed under CC BY 4.0)

The results in figure 7.2 show that smaller chunk sizes tend to extract more entity references overall. The line representing a 600-token chunk size is consistently the highest, while the 2,400-token chunk size is the lowest. This suggests that breaking text into smaller chunks allows the LLM to detect more entities compared to using larger chunks. Additionally, figure 7.2 shows that increasing the number of self-reflection iterations, meaning additional extraction passes on the same document, leads to more entity references being detected across all chunk sizes. This pattern indicates that repeated passes enable the LLM to extract more entities that may have been missed in earlier iterations.

Say you have decided to chunk the books using a 1,000-word limit (based on whitespace splitting) with an overlap of 40 words, as shown in the following listing.

Listing 7.4 Chunking the books

```
chunked_books = [chunk_text(book, 1000, 40) for book in books]
```

The books are chunked, and you can move on to the next step.

7.2.2 *Entity and relationship extraction*

The first step is to extract entities and relationships. We can borrow the MS GraphRAG prompts from the appendix of their paper. The instruction section of the prompt for entity and relationship extraction is shown in "Instructions for entity and relationship extraction."

Instructions for entity and relationship extraction

-Goal-

Given a text document that is potentially relevant to this activity and a list of entity types, identify all entities of those types from the text and all relationships among the identified entities.

-Steps-

1 Identify all entities. For each identified entity, extract the following information:
   - entity_name: Name of the entity, capitalized
   - entity_type: One of the following types: [{entity_types}]
   - entity_description: Comprehensive description of the entity's attributes and activities

   Format each entity as ("entity"{tuple_delimiter}<entity_name>{tuple_delimiter}<entity_type>{tuple_delimiter}<entity_description>)

2 From the entities identified in step 1, identify all pairs of (source_entity, target_entity) that are **clearly related** to each other. For each pair of related entities, extract the following information:
   - source_entity: name of the source entity, as identified in step 1
   - target_entity: name of the target entity, as identified in step 1
   - relationship_description: explanation as to why you think the source entity and the target entity are related to each other
   - relationship_strength: a numeric score indicating strength of the relationship between the source entity and target entity

   Format each relationship as ("relationship"{tuple_delimiter}<source_entity>{tuple_delimiter}<target_entity>{tuple_delimiter}<relationship_description>{tuple_delimiter}<relationship_strength>)

3 Return output in English as a single list of all the entities and relationships identified in steps 1 and 2. Use **{record_delimiter}** as the list delimiter.

4 When finished, output {completion_delimiter}

Instructions for entity and relationship extraction focuses on extracting structured knowledge from a text document by identifying entities of specified types and their relationships. The list of entity types is passed in as a variable `entity_types`. The prompt instructs the LLM to extract entities, classify them by type, and provide detailed descriptions. Then it identifies clearly related entity pairs, explains their connection, and assigns a relationship strength score. Finally, it returns all extracted entities and relationships in a structured, delimited format. This is only part of the full prompt, which also includes few-shot examples and output examples, but those are too extensive to include in the book.

Exercise 7.1

Before running the extraction, take a moment to consider which entity types would be most useful for *The Odyssey*. Since the list of entity types must be predefined, think about the key elements of the narrative such as characters, places, objects, and events that you want to extract. Try to define a set of entity types that would capture the most meaningful relationships in the text.

For extracting meaningful entities from *The Odyssey*, say you have decided to use the following entity types:

- `PERSON`
- `ORGANIZATION`
- `LOCATION`
- `GOD`
- `EVENT`
- `CREATURE`
- `WEAPON_OR_TOOL`

Some entity types, like `PERSON` and `GOD`, are relatively unambiguous since they refer to well-defined categories of humans and deities. However, others, like `EVENT` and `LOCATION`, are more ambiguous. An `EVENT` can refer to anything from a single action to an entire war, making it difficult to establish a strict boundary for classification. Similarly, `LOCATION` can refer to a broad category like a country, a specific city, or even a named place within a city. This variability makes consistent classification more challenging but also leaves more flexibility for the LLM.

With these predefined entity types, you will now implement the extraction function.

Listing 7.5 Entity and relationship extraction

```
 ENTITY_TYPES = ["PERSON", "ORGANIZATION", "LOCATION",
  "GOD", "EVENT", "CREATURE", "WEAPON_OR_TOOL"]
def extract_entities(text: str) -> List[Dict]:
    messages = [
        {"role": "user",
        "content": ch07_tools.create_extraction_prompt(ENTITY_TYPES, text)},
    ]
```

Selects entity types

Passes extraction prompt as user message

```
    output = chat(messages, model = "gpt-4o")          <-- LLM API call

    return ch07_tools.parse_extraction_output(output)   <-- Parses output
                                                            as a dictionary
```

The code in listing 7.5 extracts entities and relationships by first defining the entity types to be identified. It then generates an extraction prompt using these types and the input text, sends the prompt to the LLM, and processes the response into a structured dictionary format.

Using the function in listing 7.5, you will extract entities and relationships for only the first book of *The Odyssey*. If desired, you can increase the number of books to analyze a larger portion of the text. The code for this extraction is shown in the following listing.

Listing 7.6 Extracting entities and relationships

```
 number_of_books = 1
for book_i, book in enumerate(                                         Defines the
    tqdm(chunked_books[:number_of_books], desc="Processing Books")     number of books
):                                                                     to be processed
    for chunk_i, chunk in enumerate(tqdm(book, desc=f"Book {book_i}",
     leave=False)):

        nodes, relationships = extract_entities(chunk)    <-- Extracts entities
                                                              and relationships
        neo4j_driver.execute_query(                       <-- Imports entities
            ch07_tools.import_nodes_query,
            data=nodes,
            book_id=book_i,
            text=chunk,
            chunk_id=chunk_i,
        )

        neo4j_driver.execute_query(                       <-- Imports relationships
            ch07_tools.import_relationships_query,
            data=relationships
        )
```

The function in listing 7.6 processes a set number of books, extracting entities and relationships from each chunk. It then imports the entities into Neo4j, followed by their relationships, building a structured graph representation of the text.

Begin by reviewing the extracted entities and relationships. You can count the total number of entities and relationships using the code in the following listing.

Listing 7.7 Counting the number of extracted nodes and relationships

```
data, _, _ = neo4j_driver.execute_query(
    """MATCH (:`__Entity__`)
    RETURN 'entity' AS type, count(*) AS count
    UNION
```

```
    MATCH ()-[:RELATIONSHIP]->()
    RETURN 'relationship' AS type, count(*) AS count
    """
)
print([el.data() for el in data])
```

The graph contains 66 entities and 182 relationships, though these numbers may vary between executions. MS GraphRAG focuses on extracting detailed descriptions of both entities and their relationships. For example, let's examine the extracted descriptions for the character ORESTES.

Listing 7.8 Examining generated descriptions of ORESTES

```
data, _, _ = neo4j_driver.execute_query(
    """MATCH (n:PERSON)
WHERE n.name = "ORESTES"
RETURN n.description AS description"""
)
print([el.data()['description'] for el in data])
```

When examining the extracted descriptions for the character ORESTES, as shown in listing 7.8, the results might look like this:

- Orestes is Agamemnon's son who killed Aegisthus.
- Orestes is a person who was expected to take revenge on Aegisthus.
- Orestes is praised for avenging his father's murder by killing Aegisthus.
- Orestes is the son of Agamemnon who killed Aegisthus.
- Orestes is a person who was expected to take revenge on Aegisthus.
- Orestes is praised for avenging his father's murder by killing Aegisthus.

While some descriptions repeat the same facts, they collectively contain all the key details and ensure no important information is lost across different text chunks for a specific entity.

Similarly, a single pair of entities can have multiple relationships. You can explore the entity pair with the highest number of relationships using the code in the following listing.

Listing 7.9 Examining generated relationship descriptions

```
data, _, _ = neo4j_driver.execute_query(
    """MATCH (n:__Entity__)-[:RELATIONSHIP]-(m:__Entity__)
WITH n,m, count(*) AS countOfRels
ORDER BY countOfRels DESC LIMIT 1
MATCH (n)-[r:RELATIONSHIP]-(m)
RETURN n.name AS source, m.name AS target, countOfRels,
     collect(r.description) AS descriptions
"""
)
print([el.data() for el in data])
```

The entity pair with the most relationships is Telemachus and Minerva, with a total of 14 relationships. Their interactions span various moments in the narrative, highlighting Minerva's role as a divine guide and mentor to Telemachus.

The following are five of the extracted relationship descriptions:

- Telemachus spoke quietly to Minerva during the banquet.
- Minerva, in disguise, advises and encourages Telemachus, giving him courage and making him think of his father.
- Minerva brings sleep to Telemachus's mother, showing her divine influence.
- Minerva is speaking to Telemachus, offering him guidance and reassurance.
- Minerva, disguised as Mentes, is greeted by Telemachus at the gate.

While some descriptions contain overlapping details, they reinforce Minerva's role as a mentor and divine protector, gradually shaping Telemachus' journey.

7.2.3 Entity and relationship summarization

To avoid inconsistencies, redundancies, and fragmentation in the extracted knowledge, MS GraphRAG merges multiple descriptions of the same entity or relationship using LLMs to generate concise summaries. Instead of treating each description separately, the model synthesizes information from all descriptions, ensuring that key contextual details are preserved in a single, enriched representation. This approach enhances clarity, reduces duplication, and provides a more complete understanding of entities and their relationships.

Once again, you can reuse the summarization prompt from the paper, as shown in "Instructions for entity and relationship summarization."

Instructions for entity and relationship summarization

You are a helpful assistant responsible for generating a comprehensive summary of the data provided below. Given one or two entities, and a list of descriptions, all related to the same entity or group of entities. Please concatenate all of these into a single, comprehensive description. Make sure to include information collected from all the descriptions. If the provided descriptions are contradictory, please resolve the contradictions and provide a single, coherent summary. Make sure it is written in third person, and include the entity names so we have the full context.

#######

-Data-

Entities: {entity_name}

Description List: {description_list}

#######

Output:

The prompt in "Instructions for entity and relationship summarization" guides the LLM to generate a single, coherent summary by merging multiple descriptions of an entity or a pair of entities. It ensures that all relevant details are included while resolving contradictions and removing redundancies. The output is written in third person and explicitly names the entities to maintain clarity and context.

Using the prompt in "Instructions for entity and relationship summarization," you can generate summaries for all entities that have more than a single description. The code to summarize entity descriptions can be found in the following listing.

Listing 7.10 Entity summarization

```
candidates_to_summarize, _, _ = neo4j_driver.execute_query(
    """MATCH (e:__Entity__) WHERE size(e.description) > 1      ⇽ Gets all entities that have more than a single description
    RETURN e.name AS entity_name, e.description AS description_list"""
)
summaries = []
for candidate in tqdm(candidates_to_summarize, desc="Summarizing entities"):

    messages = [                                              ⇽ Constructs prompt
        {
            "role": "user",
            "content": ch07_tools.get_summarize_prompt(
                candidate["entity_name"], candidate["description_list"]
            ),
        },
    ]

    summary = chat(messages, model="gpt-4o")                 ⇽ Generates entity summary
    summaries.append(
        {"entity": candidate["entity_name"], "summary": summary}
    )
ch07_tools.import_entity_summary(neo4j_driver, summaries)
```

The code in listing 7.10 queries the Neo4j database to find entities with multiple descriptions and then uses an LLM to generate a unified summary. You can review the summarized description of `ORESTES` by running the code in the following listing.

Listing 7.11 Inspecting the generated summary for `ORESTOS`

```
summary, _, _ = neo4j_driver.execute_query(
    """MATCH (n:PERSON)
WHERE n.name = "ORESTES"
RETURN n.summary AS summary""")
print(summary[0]['summary'])
```

The results are shown in "Generated summary for ORESTES."

Generated summary for ORESTES

Orestes is the son of Agamemnon, known for avenging his father's death by killing Aegisthus. He was expected to take revenge on Aegisthus, who was responsible for Agamemnon's murder. Orestes is praised for fulfilling this expectation and successfully killing Aegisthus, his father's murderer.

The summarization process has successfully generated a cohesive and enriched description of an entity, as demonstrated by "Generated summary for ORESTES." By merging multiple descriptions, we ensure that key details are preserved while reducing redundancy.

Next, we will apply the same summarization approach to relationships, consolidating multiple relationship descriptions into a single, comprehensive summary. The results are shown in the following listing.

Listing 7.12 Relationship summarization

```
rels_to_summarize, _, _ = neo4j_driver.execute_query(
    """MATCH (s:__Entity__)-[r:RELATIONSHIP]-(t:__Entity__)    # Retrieves pairs of nodes with more than a single relationship
    WHERE id(s) < id(t)
    WITH s.name AS source, t.name AS target,
           collect(r.description) AS description_list,
           count(*) AS count
    WHERE count > 1
    RETURN source, target, description_list"""
)
rel_summaries = []
for candidate in tqdm(rels_to_summarize, desc="Summarizing relationships"):
    entity_name = f"{candidate['source']} relationship to
     {candidate['target']}"

    messages = [                                    # Constructs prompt
        {
            "role": "user",
            "content": ch07_tools.get_summarize_prompt(
                entity_name, candidate["description_list"]
            ),
        },
    ]

    summary = chat(messages, model="gpt-4o")    # Generates the relationship summary using an LLM
    rel_summaries.append({"source": candidate["source"], "target":
     candidate["target"], "summary": summary})
ch07_tools.import_rels_summary(neo4j_driver, summaries)    # Stores results to Neo4j
```

The code in listing 7.12 identifies pairs of entities in the database that share multiple relationships and consolidates their descriptions into a single summary using an LLM. By merging relationship descriptions, the process ensures that key interactions between entities are captured comprehensively while eliminating redundancy. Once generated, the summarized relationships are stored back into the database.

You can evaluate the generated relationship between TELEMACHUS and MINERVA, as shown in the following listing.

Listing 7.13 Evaluating the summarized relationship between TELEMACHUS and MINERVA

```
data, _, _ = neo4j_driver.execute_query(
    """MATCH (n:__Entity__)-[r:SUMMARIZED_RELATIONSHIP]-(m:__Entity__)
WHERE n.name = 'TELEMACHUS' AND m.name = 'MINERVA'
RETURN r.summary AS description
"""
)
print(data[0]["description"])
```

The results of code in listing 7.13 can be found in "Generated summary for relationship between TELEMACHUS and MINERVA."

Generated summary for the relationship between TELEMACHUS and MINERVA

Minerva plays a crucial role in the life of Telemachus, offering guidance and support as he embarks on his quest to find his father, Ulysses. During a banquet, Telemachus speaks quietly to Minerva, indicating a close and trusting relationship. Minerva, often in disguise, such as when she appears as Mentes, advises and encourages Telemachus, instilling in him the courage and determination to seek information about his father. She provides counsel regarding his intended voyage, demonstrating her commitment to his cause. Additionally, Minerva's divine influence is evident when she brings sleep to Telemachus's mother, further showcasing her protective and supportive role in Telemachus's life.

With the consolidated summaries for both entities and relationships, you have successfully completed the first stage of MS GraphRAG indexing. By merging information across text chunks, you have created a more coherent and enriched representation of the extracted knowledge.

Considerations for entity and relationship summarization

When working with larger datasets, you may encounter so-called super nodes. Super nodes are entities that appear in numerous chunks and have an overwhelming number of relationships. For example, if you were to process all of Ancient Greek history, a node like `Athens` would accumulate a vast number of relationships and descriptions. Without a ranking mechanism, summarizing such nodes could lead to excessively long outputs, or worse, some descriptions might not even fit within the prompt. To handle this, you would need to implement a filtering or ranking strategy to prioritize the most relevant descriptions, ensuring that the summary remains concise and informative.

Now you are ready to move on to the next stage.

7.2.4 Community detection and summarization

The second stage of the graph-indexing process focuses on community detection and summarization. A community is a group of entities that are more densely connected to each other than to the rest of the graph. Community detection results are illustrated in figure 7.3.

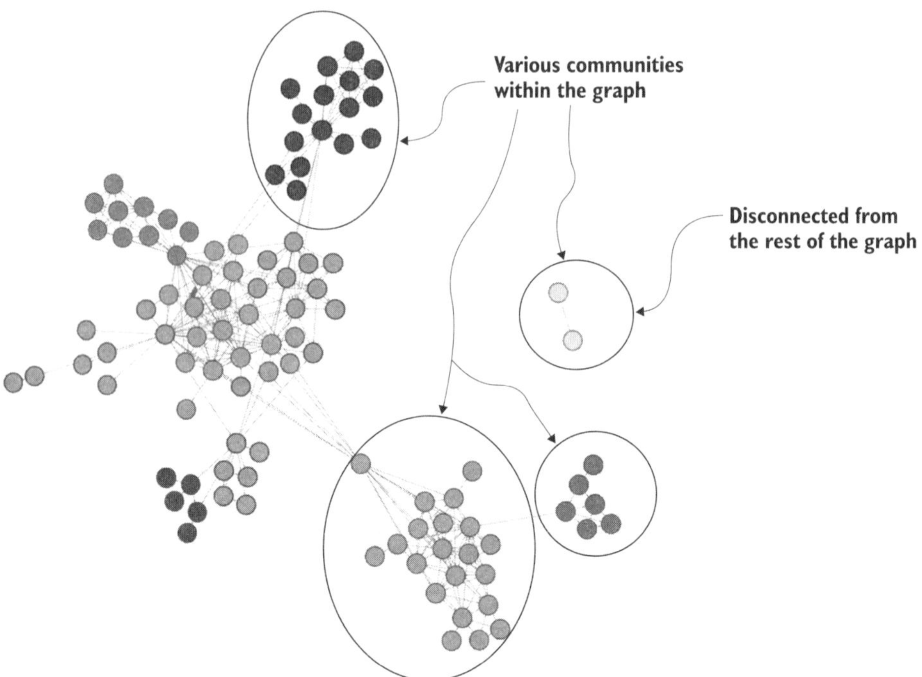

Figure 7.3 Example of community detection results

Figure 7.3 illustrates a graph where nodes are grouped into distinct communities, each representing a set of densely connected entities with stronger internal relationships. Some communities are well integrated into the overall graph, while others appear more isolated, forming disconnected subgraphs. Identifying these clusters helps reveal underlying structures, themes, or key groups within the dataset. For example, in a narrative like *The Odyssey*, a community might form around characters involved in a particular event or location. By detecting and summarizing these communities, we can capture higher-level relationships and insights that go beyond individual entity connections.

The code in listing 7.14 applies the Louvain method, a community detection algorithm, to identify groups of densely connected entities within the graph. (Leiden was used in the original paper implementation and is also available in the GDS library) The detected communities are then stored as a node property for downstream processing.

Listing 7.14 Calculating communities using the Louvain algorithm

```
community_distribution = ch07_tools.calculate_communities(neo4j_driver)
print(f"""There are {community_distribution['communityCount']} communities
     with distribution:
  {community_distribution['communityDistribution']}""")
```

The Louvain method was used to detect 9 communities in the graph, with sizes ranging from 2 to 13 nodes. The number and size of detected communities from listing 7.14 can change depending on the graph structure, such as the number of extracted entities and relationships. Additionally, Louvain is not deterministic, meaning that even with the same input, the detected communities may vary slightly between runs due to the algorithm's optimization process.

> **Hierarchical community structure**
>
> The MS GraphRAG paper uses the hierarchical nature of the Louvain algorithm to capture community structures at multiple levels of granularity. This allows for analyzing both broad and fine-grained communities within large graphs. However, since we are working with a smaller graph, we will focus on a single level of community detection and skip the hierarchical aspect.

Now you can apply the summarization prompt to generate concise overviews of each detected community. The instruction part of the prompt is available in "Instructions for community summarization."

Instructions for community summarization

You are an AI assistant that helps a human analyst to perform general information discovery. Information discovery is the process of identifying and assessing relevant information associated with certain entities (e.g., organizations and individuals) within a network.

Goal Write a comprehensive report of a community, given a list of entities that belong to the community as well as their relationships and optional associated claims. The report will be used to inform decision-makers about information associated with the community and their potential impact. The content of this report includes an overview of the community's key entities, their legal compliance, technical capabilities, reputation, and noteworthy claims.

Report Structure

The report should include the following sections:

- TITLE: community's name that represents its key entities - title should be short but specific. When possible, include representative named entities in the title.
- SUMMARY: An executive summary of the community's overall structure, how its entities are related to each other, and significant information associated with its entities.

- IMPACT SEVERITY RATING: a float score between 0-10 that represents the severity of IMPACT posed by entities within the community. IMPACT is the scored importance of a community.
- RATING EXPLANATION: Give a single sentence explanation of the IMPACT severity rating.
- DETAILED FINDINGS: A list of 5-10 key insights about the community. Each insight should have a short summary followed by multiple paragraphs of explanatory text grounded according to the grounding rules below. Be comprehensive.

The prompt in "Instructions for community summarization" guides the AI assistant in generating structured summaries of detected communities, ensuring they capture key entities, relationships, and notable insights. The goal is to produce high-quality summaries that can be effectively used downstream for RAG.

The full prompt for community summarization includes output instructions and a few-shot example to maintain consistency and relevance in the generated summaries.

With the communities identified and a structured summarization prompt in place, we can now generate comprehensive summaries for each detected community. These community summaries consolidate key entities, relationships, and significant insights.

The code in the following listing processes the detected communities and applies the summarization prompt to generate meaningful descriptions.

Listing 7.15 Generating community summaries

```
community_info, _, _ = neo4j_driver.execute_query(ch07_tools.community_info_query)   # Retrieves community information from database

communities = []
for community in tqdm(community_info, desc="Summarizing communities"):

    messages = [                                     # Constructs prompt
        {
            "role": "user",
            "content": ch07_tools.get_summarize_community_prompt(
                community["nodes"], community["rels"]
            ),
        },
    ]

    summary = chat(messages, model="gpt-4o")   # LLM call
    communities.append(
        {
            "community": json.loads(ch07_tools.extract_json(summary)),   # Parses output into dictionary
            "communityId": community["communityId"],
            "nodes": [el["id"] for el in community["nodes"]],
        }
    )
neo4j_driver.execute_query(ch07_tools.import_community_query, data=communities)   # Stores results to the database
```

You can now examine an example of a generated community summary using the code shown in listing 7.16. This will provide a concrete example of how the summarization process captures key entities, relationships, and insights within a community.

Listing 7.16 Retrieving an example community summary

```
data, _, _ = neo4j_driver.execute_query(
    """MATCH (c:__Community__)
WITH c, count {(c)<-[:IN_COMMUNITY]-()} AS size
ORDER BY size DESC LIMIT 1
RETURN c.title AS title, c.summary AS summary
"""
)
print(f"Title: {data[0]['title']})
print(f"Summary: {data[0]["summary"]}")
```

The results can be found in the "Generated summary" for relationship between TELEMACHUS and MINERVA.

Generated community summary

Minerva, Telemachus, and the Ithacan Household The community centers around Minerva, Telemachus, and the household of Ulysses, with significant interactions involving divine guidance, familial loyalty, and the challenges posed by suitors. Minerva plays a pivotal role in advising Telemachus, who is determined to find his father and restore order to his home. The relationships among these entities highlight themes of wisdom, courage, and resilience.

Handling large communities in bigger graphs

When dealing with larger graphs, communities can become too large to process efficiently. If a community contains too many entities and relationships, including all of them in the summarization prompt may exceed token limits or produce excessively long summaries. To address this, a ranking mechanism should be implemented to select only the most relevant entities and relationships. This ensures that the summary remains concise, informative, and useful for downstream RAG applications.

Congratulations! You have successfully completed the graph-indexing step.

7.3 Graph retrievers

With the graph-indexing process complete, we now move on to the graph retriever stage. This stage focuses on retrieving relevant information from the structured graph to answer queries effectively. While there are many possible retrieval strategies, we will focus on two primary approaches: local search and global search. Local search retrieves information from entities closely connected within a detected community, whereas global search considers the entire graph structure to find the most relevant information.

7.3.1 Global search

Global search in GraphRAG uses community summaries as intermediate responses to efficiently answer queries that require aggregating information across the entire dataset. Instead of retrieving individual chunks of text based on vector similarity, this method utilizes precomputed community-level summaries to generate a structured response. A global search search diagram is visualized in figure 7.4.

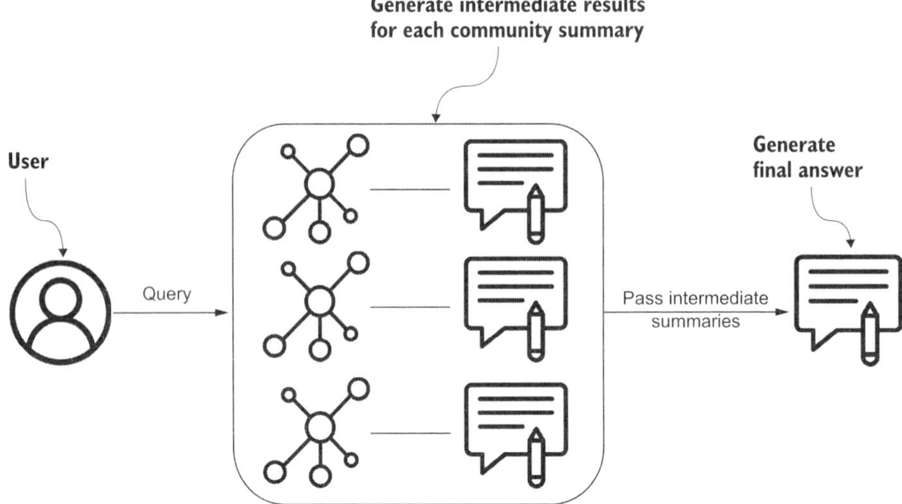

Figure 7.4 Global search

The process in figure 7.4 follows a map-reduce approach:

- *Map step*—Given a user query and, optionally, the conversation history, GraphRAG retrieves LLM-generated community reports from a specified level in the graph's community hierarchy. In your implementation, the graph is structured with a single level of communities, meaning all detected groups exist at the same hierarchical depth. These reports are segmented into manageable text chunks, and each chunk is processed by the LLM to produce an intermediate response. Each response consists of a list of key points, each accompanied by a numerical importance rating.
- *Reduce step*—The most important points across all intermediate responses are filtered and aggregated. These refined insights then serve as the final context for the LLM, which synthesizes a cohesive answer to the user query. By structuring the dataset into semantically meaningful clusters, GraphRAG enables efficient and cohesive retrieval, even for broad, thematic queries.

The map step uses the following system prompt, as shown in "The system prompt for the map part of the retriever."

Community hierarchy structure

The quality of the response depends on the level of the community hierarchy chosen for sourcing community reports. Lower-level communities provide detailed reports, leading to more thorough responses, but they also increase the number of LLM calls and processing time. Higher-level communities, with more abstracted summaries, may be more efficient but risk losing granularity. Balancing detail and efficiency is key to optimizing global search performance.

The system prompt for the map part of the retriever

—Role—

You are a helpful assistant responding to questions about data in the tables provided.

—Goal—

Generate a response consisting of a list of key points that responds to the user's question, summarizing all relevant information in the input data tables.

You should use the data provided in the data tables below as the primary context for generating the response. If you don't know the answer or if the input data tables do not contain sufficient information to provide an answer, just say so. Do not make anything up.

Each key point in the response should have the following element:

- Description: A comprehensive description of the point.
- Importance Score: An integer score between 0-100 that indicates how important the point is in answering the user's question. An 'I don't know' type of response should have a score of 0.

The response should be JSON formatted as follows: {{ "points": [{{"description": "Description of point 1 [Data: Reports (report ids)]", "score": score_value}}, {{"description": "Description of point 2 [Data: Reports (report ids)]", "score": score_value}}] }}

The response shall preserve the original meaning and use of modal verbs such as "shall", "may" or "will".

Points supported by data should list the relevant reports as references as follows: "This is an example sentence supported by data references [Data: Reports (report ids)]"

Do not list more than 5 record ids in a single reference. Instead, list the top 5 most relevant record ids and add "+more" to indicate that there are more.

For example: "Person X is the owner of Company Y and subject to many allegations of wrongdoing [Data: Reports (2, 7, 64, 46, 34, +more)]. He is also CEO of company X [Data: Reports (1, 3)]"

where 1, 2, 3, 7, 34, 46, and 64 represent the id (not the index) of the relevant data report in the provided tables.

Do not include information where the supporting evidence for it is not provided.

—Data tables—

{context_data}

The map system prompt instructs the LLM to extract key points from the provided context in response to a user query. Each key point includes a description and an importance score (0–100) reflecting its relevance to the query. The response is formatted as JSON, with references to supporting data report IDs. If insufficient information is available, the response must indicate so without speculation.

Now you will examine the reduce step of the retriever, as shown in "The system prompt for the reduce part of the retriever."

The system prompt for the reduce part of the retriever

—Role—

You are a helpful assistant responding to questions about a dataset by synthesizing perspectives from multiple analysts.

—Goal—

Generate a response of the target length and format that responds to the user's question, summarize all the reports from multiple analysts who focused on different parts of the dataset.

Note that the analysts' reports provided below are ranked in the **descending order of importance**.

If you don't know the answer or if the provided reports do not contain sufficient information to provide an answer, just say so. Do not make anything up.

The final response should remove all irrelevant information from the analysts' reports and merge the cleaned information into a comprehensive answer that provides explanations of all the key points and implications appropriate for the response length and format.

Add sections and commentary to the response as appropriate for the length and format. Style the response in markdown.

The response shall preserve the original meaning and use of modal verbs such as "shall", "may" or "will".

The response should also preserve all the data references previously included in the analysts' reports, but do not mention the roles of multiple analysts in the analysis process.

Do not list more than 5 record ids in a single reference. Instead, list the top 5 most relevant record ids and add "+more" to indicate that there are more.

For example:

"Person X is the owner of Company Y and subject to many allegations of wrongdoing [Data: Reports (2, 7, 34, 46, 64, +more)]. He is also CEO of company X [Data: Reports (1, 3)]"

where 1, 2, 3, 7, 34, 46, and 64 represent the id (not the index) of the relevant data record.

Do not include information where the supporting evidence for it is not provided.

—Target response length and format—

{response_type}

The reduce system prompt directs the LLM to synthesize key points from multiple analyst reports, which are ranked by importance. The response must be formatted in Markdown, be structured appropriately for the target length and format, and exclude irrelevant details. It preserves all referenced data while avoiding speculative answers. The final output integrates and refines insights from the reports into a coherent, comprehensive response.

Now we can combine the map and reduce prompts into a global search function.

Listing 7.17 Global search

```
def global_retriever(query: str, rating_threshold: float = 5) -> str:

    community_data, _, _ = neo4j_driver.execute_query(     # Gets all communities above the rating threshold
        """
    MATCH (c:__Community__)
    WHERE c.rating >= $rating
    RETURN c.summary AS summary
    """,
        rating=rating_threshold,
    )
    print(f"Got {len(community_data)} community summaries")
    intermediate_results = []
    for community in tqdm(community_data, desc="Processing communities"):

        intermediate_messages = [     # For each community, gets an intermediate response
            {
                "role": "system",
                "content":
     ch07_tools.get_map_system_prompt(community["summary"]),
            },
            {
                "role": "user",
                "content": query,
            },
        ]
```

```
        intermediate_response = chat(intermediate_messages, model="gpt-4o")
        intermediate_results.append(intermediate_response)

    final_messages = [                                          <-- Generates a final answer
        {                                                           using all the intermediate
            "role": "system",                                       responses as context
            "content":
     ch07_tools.get_reduce_system_prompt(intermediate_results),
        },
        {"role": "user", "content": query},
    ]
    summary = chat(final_messages, model="gpt-4o")
    return summary
```

The `global_retriever` function in listing 7.17 implements the global search method by using community summaries to generate a structured response. It follows a three-step process:

1. *Retrieve relevant communities*—The function queries a Neo4j database to retrieve community summaries where the rating meets or exceeds the specified threshold. This ensures that only the most relevant communities contribute to the final answer.
2. *Generate intermediate responses*—For each community, an intermediate response is generated using the map system prompt. The model processes the community summary alongside the user's query to extract key points.
3. *Aggregate and generate final answer*—The reduce system prompt is then applied to synthesize all intermediate responses into a coherent final answer, ensuring that the most important points are retained and properly structured.

Now we can test this function with an example.

Listing 7.18 Global search example

```
print(global_retriever("What is this story about?"))
```

The results of the listing 7.18 can be found in "Response for 'What is this story about?' using global search."

Response for 'What is this story about?' using global search

The story revolves around the intricate dynamics of a community involving key figures such as Minerva, Telemachus, and the household of Ulysses. Central themes include divine guidance, familial loyalty, and the challenges posed by suitors. Minerva plays a crucial role in advising Telemachus, who is determined to find his father, Ulysses, and restore order to his home. The relationships among the characters emphasize themes of wisdom, courage, and resilience.

Additionally, the narrative highlights the role of Mentes, the chief of the Taphians, who is recognized as the son of Anchialus. Mentes is involved in a voyage to Temesa, known for its iron cargo, and claims kingship over the Taphians [Data: Reports (1)]. The story also centers around Odysseus, a key figure in Greek mythology, and his connections with other significant entities such as the Achaeans, Laertes, and the gods. The relationships in the story underscore the impact of divine intervention on human affairs, showcasing how the gods influence the lives of Greek heroes [Data: Reports (1, 2, 3, 4, 5)].

Furthermore, the narrative explores the mythological elements involving Olympian Jove, Aegisthus, Agamemnon, Orestes, and Mercury. It highlights themes of divine intervention, betrayal, and vengeance. Olympian Jove discusses the actions of Aegisthus, notorious for his betrayal and murder of Agamemnon, while Orestes avenges his father's death by killing Aegisthus, despite warnings from Mercury [Data: Reports (1, 2, 3, 4, 5)]. These interconnected stories weave a rich tapestry of mythological and heroic elements, emphasizing the enduring legacy and challenges faced by these legendary figures.

The response in "Response for 'What is this story about?' using global search" generated by the global search method provides a structured summary of the story by synthesizing key themes and relationships from multiple chunks. It highlights the central figures Minerva, Telemachus, and Ulysses—along with their roles in the narrative, emphasizing divine guidance, familial loyalty, and challenges faced by the household of Ulysses.

Exercise 7.2

Try running different types of queries using the global search function. Ask broad questions that require synthesizing information across multiple community summaries, such as "What are the central conflicts in this story?"

7.3.2 *Local search*

The local search method enhances LLM responses by combining structured knowledge graph data with unstructured text from source documents. This approach is particularly effective for entity-focused queries, such as "What are the healing properties of chamomile?" where a deep understanding of a specific entity and its relationships is required. The local search approach can be found in figure 7.5.

When a user submits a query, the system visualized in figure 7.5 first identifies semantically related entities within the knowledge graph using vector search. These entities act as entry points for retrieving relevant information, including directly connected entities, relationships, and summaries from community reports. Additionally, text chunks from the input documents associated with these entities are also extracted. The retrieved data is ranked and filtered to fit within a constrained

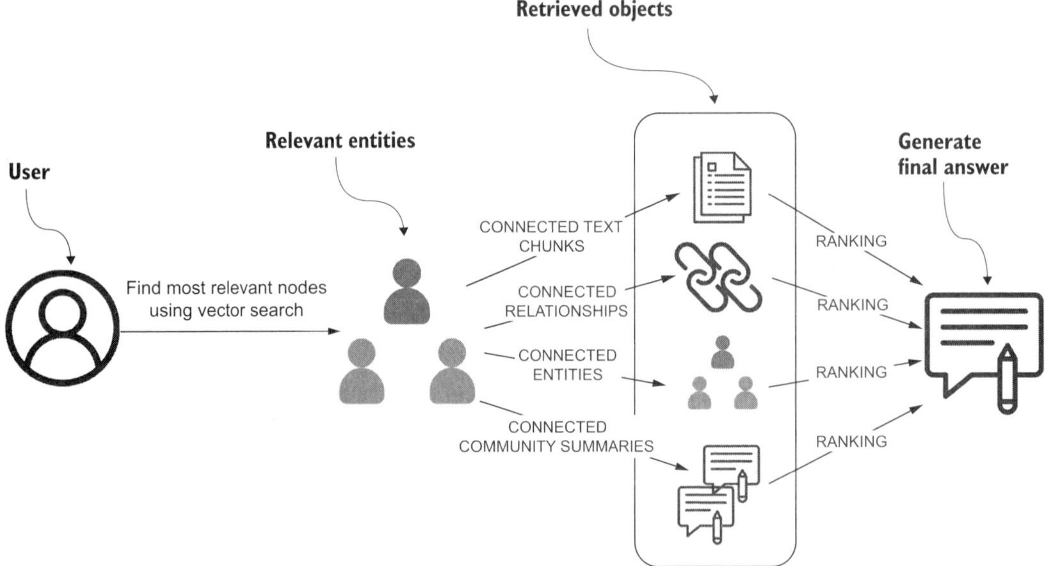

Figure 7.5 Local search

context window, ensuring that only the most relevant information is included in the final response.

To implement local search, we first need to calculate text embeddings for entities and create a vector index. This allows us to efficiently retrieve the most relevant entities based on the user's query. By embedding entity descriptions and relationships into a vector space, we can use similarity search to identify which entities are most closely related to the input. Once these relevant entities are found, they serve as entry points for retrieving additional structured and unstructured data. The code for computing these embeddings and constructing the vector index is shown in the following listing.

Listing 7.19 Generate text embeddings for all entities in the database

```
entities, _, _ = neo4j_driver.execute_query(
    """
MATCH (e:__Entity__)
RETURN e.summary AS summary, e.name AS name
"""
)
data = [{"name": el["name"], "embedding": embed(el["summary"])[0]} for el in
     entities]
neo4j_driver.execute_query(
    """
UNWIND $data AS row
MATCH (e:__Entity__ {name: row.name})
CALL db.create.setNodeVectorProperty(e, 'embedding', row.embedding)
```

- Retrieves entities and their summaries
- Calculates embeddings based on entity summaries
- Stores embeddings to the database

```
""",
    data=data,
)
neo4j_driver.execute_query(
    """
CREATE VECTOR INDEX entities IF NOT EXISTS
FOR (n:__Entity__)
ON (n.embedding)
""",
    data=data,
)
```

Creates vector index entities

The code in listing 7.19 retrieves all entities from the database along with their summaries, computes text embeddings for each entity based on its summary, and stores the embeddings back into the database. Finally, it creates a vector index to enable efficient similarity search on entity embeddings.

The local search is finally implemented as a Cypher statement that expands the initial set of relevant nodes, identified through vector search, to include their connected entities, text chunks, summaries, and relationships. This Cypher statement is shown in the following listing.

Listing 7.20 Cypher statement for local search

```
local_search_query = """
CALL db.index.vector.queryNodes('entities', $k, $embedding)
YIELD node, score
WITH collect(node) as nodes
WITH collect {
    UNWIND nodes as n
    MATCH (n)<-[:HAS_ENTITY]->(c:__Chunk__)
    WITH c, count(distinct n) as freq
    RETURN c.text AS chunkText
    ORDER BY freq DESC
    LIMIT $topChunks
} AS text_mapping,
collect {
    UNWIND nodes as n
    MATCH (n)-[:IN_COMMUNITY]->(c:__Community__)
    WITH c, c.rank as rank, c.weight AS weight
    RETURN c.summary
    ORDER BY rank, weight DESC
    LIMIT $topCommunities
} AS report_mapping,
collect {
    UNWIND nodes as n
    MATCH (n)-[r:SUMMARIZED_RELATIONSHIP]-(m)
    WHERE m IN nodes
    RETURN r.summary AS descriptionText
    ORDER BY r.rank, r.weight DESC
    LIMIT $topInsideRels
} as insideRels,
collect {
    UNWIND nodes as n
```

Fetches related text chunks

Fetches related community descriptions

Fetches related relationships

Fetches entity summaries

```
    RETURN n.summary AS descriptionText
} as entities
RETURN {Chunks: text_mapping, Reports: report_mapping,
       Relationships: insideRels,
       Entities: entities} AS text
"""
```

All retrieved objects in listing 7.20, such as text chunks, community descriptions, relationships, and entity summaries, are ranked and limited to ensure the prompt remains manageable. Text chunks are ranked by how frequently they are associated with relevant entities and limited to the top `topChunks`. Community descriptions are ordered by rank and weight, selecting only the `topCommunities`. Relationships are ranked by their importance and limited to `topInsideRels`. Finally, entity summaries are retrieved without additional ranking constraints. This ensures only the most relevant information is included in the response.

Lastly, you need to define the summarizing prompt, which is again borrowed from the paper and shown in "The system prompt for the local search."

The system prompt for the local search

—Role—

You are a helpful assistant responding to questions about data in the tables provided.

—Goal—

Generate a response of the target length and format that responds to the user's question, summarizing all information in the input data tables appropriate for the response length and format, and incorporating any relevant general knowledge.

If you don't know the answer, just say so. Do not make anything up.

Points supported by data should list their data references as follows:

"This is an example sentence supported by multiple data references [Data: <dataset name> (record ids); <dataset name> (record ids)]."

Do not list more than 5 record ids in a single reference. Instead, list the top 5 most relevant record ids and add "+more" to indicate that there are more.

For example:

"Person X is the owner of Company Y and subject to many allegations of wrongdoing [Data: Sources (15, 16), Reports (1), Entities (5, 7); Relationships (23); Claims (2, 7, 34, 46, 64, +more)]."

where 15, 16, 1, 5, 7, 23, 2, 7, 34, 46, and 64 represent the id (not the index) of the relevant data record.

Do not include information where the supporting evidence for it is not provided.

—Target response length and format—

{response_type}

—Data tables—

{context_data}

This system prompt in "The system prompt for the local search" is designed to generate responses based on structured data tables while maintaining accuracy and transparency. It instructs the assistant to synthesize information relevant to the user's query, ensuring that claims are supported by explicit data references. The format for citing data sources enforces a structured approach, limiting the number of record IDs per reference while indicating additional supporting records when applicable. The prompt also emphasizes that if an answer is not found in the provided data, the assistant should explicitly state so rather than fabricate information.

With this in place, you can now implement local search.

Listing 7.21 Local search implementation

```
def local_search(query: str) -> str:

    context, _, _ = neo4j_driver.execute_query(        ◁ Fetches context using
        local_search_query,                                the local search
        embedding=embed(query)[0],                         Cypher statement
        topChunks=topChunks,
        topCommunities=topCommunities,
        topInsideRels=topInsideRels,
        k=k_entities,
    )

    context_str = str(context[0]["text"])      ◁ Stringifies context

    local_messages = [                      ◁ Constructs prompt
        {
            "role": "system",
            "content": ch07_tools.get_local_system_prompt(context_str),
        },
        {
            "role": "user",
            "content": query,
        },
    ]                                                          Generates
                                                               final
    final_answer = chat(local_messages, model="gpt-4o")     ◁ answer
    return final_answer
```

Listing 7.21 implements local search by first retrieving relevant context from the knowledge graph using vector search and the Cypher query. The extracted context is then converted into a string and incorporated into a structured prompt designed to guide the LLM in generating an informed response. Finally, the prompt is sent to the model to produce the final answer.

You can now test this implementation with an example.

Listing 7.22 Local search implementation

```
print(local_search("Who is Ulysses?"))
```

The results of the listing 7.22 can be found in "Response for 'Who is Ulysses?' using local search."

Response for "Who is Ulysses?" using local search

The story revolves around the intricate dynamics of a community involving key figures such as Minerva, Telemachus, and the household of Ulysses. Central themes include divine guidance, familial loyalty, and the challenges posed by suitors. Minerva plays a crucial role in advising Telemachus, who is determined to find his father, Ulysses, and restore order to his home. The relationships among the characters emphasize themes of wisdom, courage, and resilience.

Additionally, the narrative highlights the role of Mentes, the chief of the Taphians, who is recognized as the son of Anchialus. Mentes is involved in a voyage to Temesa, known for its iron cargo, and claims kingship over the Taphians [Data: Reports (1)]. The story also centers around Odysseus, a key figure in Greek mythology, and his connections with other significant entities such as the Achaeans, Laertes, and the gods. The relationships in the story underscore the impact of divine intervention on human affairs, showcasing how the gods influence the lives of Greek heroes [Data: Reports (1, 2, 3, 4, 5)].

Furthermore, the narrative explores the mythological elements involving Olympian Jove, Aegisthus, Agamemnon, Orestes, and Mercury. It highlights themes of divine intervention, betrayal, and vengeance. Olympian Jove discusses the actions of Aegisthus, notorious for his betrayal and murder of Agamemnon, while Orestes avenges his father's death by killing Aegisthus, despite warnings from Mercury [Data: Reports (1, 2, 3, 4, 5)]. These interconnected stories weave a rich tapestry of mythological and heroic elements, emphasizing the enduring legacy and challenges faced by these legendary figures.

The response in "Response for 'Who is Ulysses?' using local search" demonstrates how local search retrieves and synthesizes relevant information from the knowledge graph to provide a detailed, well-supported answer. By incorporating connected entities, relationships, and community summaries, the system ensures that responses capture both narrative context and factual depth.

Exercise 7.3

Try running different types of queries using the local search function.

With such a graph index, different retriever strategies can be implemented. For example, community summaries could be embedded separately and used as a standalone vector retriever, allowing for more targeted retrieval depending on the query's focus.

Congratulations! You have successfully implemented complete MS GraphRAG.

Summary

- MS GraphRAG uses a two-stage process where entities and relationships are first extracted and summarized from source documents, followed by community detection and summarization to create a cohesive knowledge representation.
- The extraction process uses LLMs to identify entities, classify them by predefined types (e.g., `PERSON`, `GOD`, `LOCATION`), and generate detailed descriptions of both entities and their relationships, including relationship strength scores.
- Entity and relationship descriptions from multiple text chunks are consolidated through LLM-based summarization to create unified, nonredundant representations that preserve key information.
- The system detects communities of densely connected entities using algorithms like the Louvain method and then generates community-level summaries to capture higher-level themes and relationships.
- Global search uses community summaries to answer broad, thematic queries through a map-reduce approach.
- Local search combines vector similarity search with graph traversal to answer entity-focused queries.
- The effectiveness of retrieval depends on factors like chunk size, entity type selection, and community detection parameters, with smaller chunks generally leading to more comprehensive entity extraction.
- The system handles potential scaling challenges through ranking mechanisms for managing large numbers of entities, relationships, and communities while maintaining context relevance.

8 RAG application evaluation

This chapter covers

- Benchmarking RAG applications and agent capabilities
- Designing evaluation datasets
- Applying RAGAS metrics: recall, faithfulness, correctness

In this chapter, you will explore the importance of evaluating your RAG application performance using carefully constructed benchmark questions. As your RAG pipeline grows more sophisticated and complex, it becomes essential to ensure that your agent's answers remain both accurate and coherent across a wide range of queries. A benchmark evaluation provides the system needed to measure the agent's capabilities while also helping to clearly define and scope the agent.

Evaluating RAG applications involves multiple approaches, each addressing different steps of the application, as shown in figure 8.1, which illustrates a high-level overview of a pipeline for a question-answering system powered by an LLM with retrieval capabilities. It begins with the user posing a question to the system. The LLM then identifies the most suitable retrieval tool to fetch the necessary information. This step is critical and can be evaluated for the accuracy of the tool selection process.

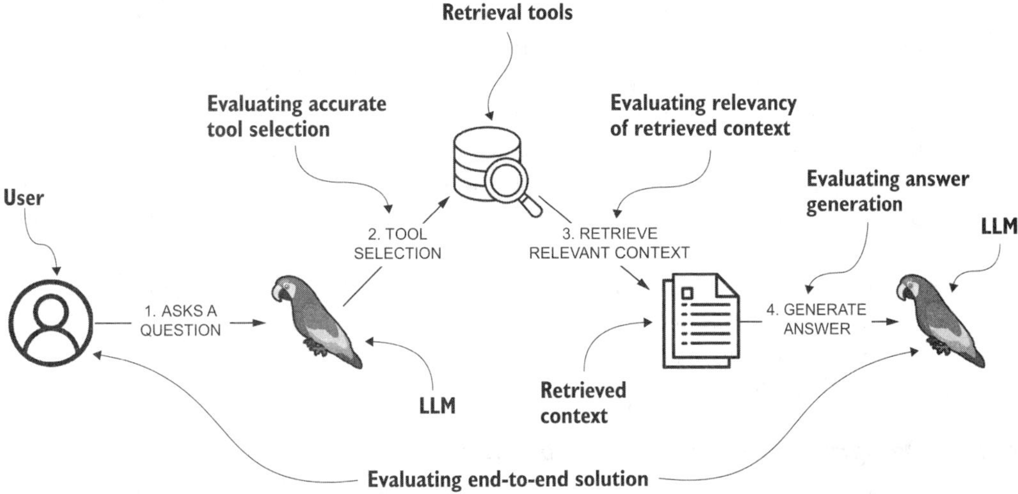

Figure 8.1 Evaluating different steps of a RAG pipeline

Throughout this book, you have implemented various retrieval tool designs, starting with vector search and progressing to more structured approaches like text2cypher and Cypher templates. Each retrieval method serves different needs:

- Vector search efficiently retrieves semantically relevant documents.
- Cypher templates allow precise, structured queries to databases.
- Text2cypher allows dynamic and flexible querying, benefiting from the expressive power of graph-based retrieval.

Evaluating which tool the LLM selects and how well it matches the query's needs is crucial for optimizing retrieval performance.

Once the appropriate tool is chosen, it retrieves relevant context or data from a knowledge base. The relevance of this retrieved context to the user's question is another key evaluation point. A well-chosen retrieval method should ensure that the fetched context is both accurate and sufficient for answering the query.

Using the retrieved context, the LLM generates an answer, which is then presented to the user. At this stage, we can assess not only the coherence and accuracy of the generated response but also the model's ability to understand and integrate the provided context effectively. A particularly important evaluation criterion is whether the LLM produces the correct answer when given the correct context. This allows us to measure the model's reasoning and synthesis capabilities separately from retrieval performance.

Additionally, the entire pipeline can be evaluated holistically to measure its effectiveness in providing accurate and contextually relevant answers to user queries. By analyzing failures at different stages—tool selection, retrieval relevance, and final response generation—we can iteratively improve both the retrieval mechanisms and the LLM's ability to utilize retrieved information.

Say you are responsible for evaluating the performance of the LLM agent implemented in chapter 5. To gain deeper insight into its effectiveness, you will use the RAGAS Python library to design and conduct a benchmark analysis. But first, you need to design the benchmark dataset. In the remainder of this chapter, we'll move from concepts to code and walk through the implementation step by step. To follow along, you'll need access to a running Neo4j instance. This can be a local installation or a cloud-hosted instance. In the implementation of this chapter, we use what we call the "Movies dataset." See the appendix for more information on the dataset and various ways to load it. You can follow the implementation directly in the accompanying Jupyter notebook available here: https://github.com/tomasonjo/kg-rag/blob/main/notebooks/ch08.ipynb.

Let's dive in.

8.1 Designing the benchmark dataset

Creating a benchmark dataset requires designing input queries that test various aspects of the system's decision making and response generation. Since each step in the RAG pipeline plays a vital role, the dataset should include diverse questions that challenge different components:

- *Tool selection evaluation*—Ssome queries should evaluate whether the system selects the correct retrieval method, ensuring it identifies the most relevant source of information.
- *Entity and value mapping*—Other queries might focus on testing specific tasks, such as mapping entities or values from user input to the corresponding entries in a database.
- *Multistep retrieval scenarios*—Some agents have the ability to execute multiple retrieval steps, where the initially retrieved data serves as input for a second retrieval step. The benchmark should include cases where the system needs to refine or expand upon the first retrieval to fully answer the query. These cases are particularly important for answering complex questions that depend on dynamically chaining multiple queries.
- *Edge cases and functional coverage*—To fully understand system performance, the benchmark must cover all functionalities and known edge cases. This includes handling ambiguous queries, long-tail concepts, and scenarios where multiple retrieval methods might be applicable.
- *Conversational usability*—Additionally, it may be useful to evaluate the agent's ability to handle greetings, clarify ambiguous queries, and effectively communicate its capabilities to ensure a smooth and user-friendly experience.

By systematically benchmarking these aspects, we gain a clearer understanding of how well the agent performs under different conditions. This allows for targeted improvements, ensuring robustness and reliability in real-world deployments.

8.1.1 Coming up with test examples

To evaluate the system comprehensively, you need well-defined end-to-end test examples. Each example consists of a question and its corresponding ground truth response, as shown in figure 8.2, ensuring that the system's output can be reliably assessed.

Question	Ground truth
How many movies did Tom Hanks appear in?	12
Which is the highest-rated comedy?	George Carlin: Jammin' in New York

Figure 8.2 Benchmark test example

Instead of providing a static string as the expected answer, we can use Cypher queries to define the ground truth dynamically. Since we are dealing with a graph database, this approach offers a significant advantage: even if the underlying data changes, the benchmark remains valid. This ensures that test cases, as shown in figure 8.3, remain accurate over time without requiring constant updates.

Question	Ground truth
How many movies did Tom Hanks appear in?	`MATCH (p:Person {name: "Tom Hanks"})-[:ACTED_IN]->(m:Movie) RETURN count(m) AS moviesCount`
Which is the highest-rated comedy?	`MATCH (m:Movie)-[:IN_GENRE]->(g:Genre {name: "Comedy"}) WHERE m.imdbRating IS NOT NULL RETURN m.title, m.imdbRating ORDER BY m.imdbRating DESC LIMIT 1`

Figure 8.3 Benchmark test example with a Cypher statement as ground truth

When designing a benchmark dataset, you should include diverse examples to evaluate different aspects of the agent's performance. For instance, you can evaluate how the agent responds to greetings like "Hello," provides guidance to the user, or handles irrelevant queries, as demonstrated in table 8.1.

This table provides examples of how the agent responds to simple greetings, user guidance requests, and irrelevant queries. It shows how you can use a simple `RETURN`

Table 8.1 Benchmark examples that test simple greetings and irrelevant questions

Question	Cypher
Hello	`RETURN "greeting and reminder it can only answer questions related to movies."`
What can you do?	`RETURN "answer questions related to movies and their cast."`
What is the weather like in Spain?	`RETURN "irrelevant question as we can answer questions related to movies and their cast only."`

Cypher statement to define static answers that don't need to look for information in the database. For example, when greeted with "Hello," the agent replies with a greeting and a reminder of its scope. If asked what it can do, it clarifies that it answers questions about movies and their casts. For unrelated queries, like about the weather, the agent simply states that it only handles movie-related questions.

Next, we can define a set of questions to evaluate both tool usage and the LLM's ability to generate accurate answers using those tools. The examples are shown in table 8.2.

Table 8.2 Benchmark examples that test tools usage and value mapping

Question	Cypher
Who acted in Top Gun?	`RETURN "MATCH (p:Person)-[:ACTED_IN]->(m:Movie {title: "Top Gun"}) RETURN p.name"`
Who acted in top gun?	`RETURN "MATCH (p:Person)-[:ACTED_IN]->(m:Movie {title: "Top Gun"}) RETURN p.name"`
In which movies did Tom Hanks act in?	`MATCH (p:Person {name: "Tom Hanks"})-[:ACTED_IN]->(m:Movie) RETURN m.title`
In which movies did tom Hanks act in?	`MATCH (p:Person {name: "Tom Hanks"})-[:ACTED_IN]->(m:Movie) RETURN m.title`

The examples in table 8.2 demonstrate cases where the LLM needs to retrieve relevant data from the database using available tools. Here, the LLM should utilize two key tools: one for finding movies by actor and another for finding actors by movie, ensuring fast and reliable responses.

Additionally, these examples allow us to evaluate how well the agent maps user input to database values. For well-known movies and actors, the LLM often generates correct queries out of the box based on its pretraining. However, for lesser-known or private datasets, a dedicated mapping system is essential for accurate entity resolution. Implementing such a system ensures that user inputs are correctly linked to database entries, improving both accuracy and reliability.

You should also include some examples where the LLM will need to use the text2-cypher tool, as shown in table 8.3.

Table 8.3 Benchmark examples that test queries involving aggregations and filtering

Question	Cypher
Who acted in the most movies?	`MATCH (p:Person)-[:ACTED_IN]->(m:Movie) RETURN p.name, COUNT(m) AS movieCount ORDER BY movieCount DESC LIMIT 1`
List people born before 1940.	`MATCH (p:Person) WHERE p.born < 1940 RETURN p.name`
Who was born in 1965 and has directed a movie?	`MATCH (p:Person)-[:DIRECTED]->(m:Movie) WHERE p.born = 1965 RETURN p.name`

Table 8.3 includes queries that involve aggregations, filtering, and relationships, such as finding the actor with the most movie roles, listing people born before a certain year, and identifying directors born in a specific year. Since no dedicated tool is implemented to handle these queries, the LLM must rely on text2cypher to construct the appropriate Cypher statements based on the provided graph schema.

You should also test edge cases, such as queries where relevant data is missing but still within the domain, as demonstrated in table 8.4.

Table 8.4 Benchmark examples that test questions where data is missing

Question	Cypher
Which movie has the most Oscars?	`RETURN "This information is missing"`

The benchmark will be very dependent on the functionalities of your agent. The specific capabilities, such as retrieval strategies, reasoning methods, and structured output handling, will influence the benchmark's effectiveness in assessing performance. When designing a benchmark, it is crucial to ensure comprehensive coverage of your agent's functionalities. By incorporating a variety of examples, you can effectively test how well your agent handles different challenges.

The benchmark has 17 examples in total, with some not shown here. You can now evaluate them.

8.2 Evaluation

To assess the performance of your benchmark, you will use RAGAS, a framework designed for evaluating RAG systems. As mentioned, the evaluation focuses on three key metrics, discussed next.

8.2.1 Context recall

Context recall measures how many relevant pieces of information were successfully retrieved using the prompt in "Context recall evaluation." A high score indicates that the retrieval system effectively captures all necessary context needed to answer the query.

Context recall evaluation

Goal: Given a context and an answer, analyze each sentence in the answer and classify whether the sentence can be attributed to the given context or not. Use only 'Yes' (1) or 'No' (0) as a binary classification. Output JSON with reasoning.

The prompt in "Context recall evaluation" ensures that every sentence in the generated answer is explicitly supported by the retrieved context. By doing so, it helps evaluate how effectively the retrieval system captures relevant information.

Next, the faithfulness assessment ensures that the generated response remains factually aligned with the retrieved content.

8.2.2 *Faithfulness*

Faithfulness evaluates whether the generated response remains factually consistent with the retrieved context. A response is considered faithful if all its claims can be directly supported by the provided documents, minimizing the risk of hallucination. Faithfulness is assessed using a two-step process. In the first step, it decomposes the answer into atomic statements using the prompt in "Faithfulness statement breakdown," ensuring that each unit of information is clear and self-contained, making verification easier.

Faithfulness statement breakdown

Goal: Given a question and an answer, analyze the complexity of each sentence in the answer. Break down each sentence into one or more fully understandable statements. Ensure that no pronouns are used in any statement. Format the outputs in JSON.

Once the statements are generated, it evaluates their faithfulness using the prompt in "Faithfulness evaluation."

Faithfulness evaluation

Goal: Your task is to judge the faithfulness of a series of statements based on a given context. For each statement, return a verdict as 1 if the statement can be directly inferred from the context or 0 if the statement cannot be directly inferred from the context.

The prompt in "Faithfulness evaluation" checks whether the statements in the generated response are factually grounded in the retrieved context. It ensures that the model does not introduce unsupported claims.

Finally, we evaluate answer correctness by comparing the generated response with the ground truth.

8.2.3 *Answer correctness*

Answer correctness assesses how accurately and completely the response addresses the user's query. It considers both factual accuracy and relevance to ensure the response aligns with the intent of the question. Answer correctness uses the same process as faithfulness to generate statements and then evaluates them using the prompt in "Answer correctness evaluation."

Answer correctness evaluation

Goal: Given a ground truth and an answer statement, analyze each statement and classify it into one of the following categories:

TP (true positive): Statements present in the answer that are also directly supported by one or more statements in the ground truth. FP (false positive): Statements present in the answer but not directly supported by any statement in the ground truth. FN (false negative): Statements found in the ground truth but not present in the answer.

Each statement can only belong to one of these categories. Provide a reason for each classification.

The prompt in "Answer correctness evaluation" ensures that the response is both factually correct and aligned with the expected answer by systematically comparing the generated statements with the ground truth.

By analyzing these metrics, you can determine how well the system retrieves relevant data, maintains factual consistency, and generates correct responses. This evaluation will help identify potential weaknesses, such as missing context, inconsistencies, or inaccurate answers, allowing for iterative refinement and improved performance.

8.2.4 Loading the dataset

The benchmark dataset is provided as a CSV file in the accompanying repository, making it easy to load and use, as demonstrated in the following listing.

Listing 8.1 Loading benchmark dataset from CSV

```
test_data = pd.read_csv("../data/benchmark_data.csv", delimiter=";")
```

8.2.5 Running evaluation

To evaluate the system's performance, you will generate answers for the benchmark dataset and compare them against the expected ground truth responses. First, you need to obtain the ground truth by executing the corresponding Cypher statements and generating answers using the agent, as shown in listing 8.2. Additionally, you must record latency and retrieved contexts to analyze the system's efficiency and relevance.

Listing 8.2 Generating answers and ground truth responses

```
answers = []
ground_truths = []
latencies = []
contexts = []
```

```
for i, row in tqdm(test_data.iterrows(), total=len(test_data),
     desc="Processing rows"):
    ground_truth, _, _ = neo4j_driver.execute_query(row["cypher"])
    ground_truths.append([str(el.data()) for el in ground_truth])
    start = datetime.now()
    try:
        answer, context = get_answer(row["question"])
        context = [el['content'] for el in context]
    except Exception:
        answer, context = None, []
    latencies.append((datetime.now() - start).total_seconds())
    answers.append(answer)
    contexts.append(context)

test_data['ground_truth'] = [str(el) for el in ground_truths]
test_data['answer'] = answers
test_data['latency'] = latencies
test_data['retrieved_contexts'] = contexts
```

The provided Cypher statement returns the ground truth.

Executes the agent to generate a response to the question

Calculates the latency

Stores the results back to the dataframe

Now that we have collected all the necessary input data, including generated answers and ground truth responses, we can proceed with the evaluation.

Listing 8.3 Evaluating the generated answer and retrieved context

```
dataset = Dataset.from_pandas(test_data.fillna("I don't know"))

result = evaluate(
    dataset,

    metrics=[
        answer_correctness,
        context_recall,
        faithfulness,
    ],
)
```

Changes missing response answers to "I don't know"

Runs the evaluation using RAGAS framework

Relevant metrics

This code in listing 8.3 runs the evaluation using the RAGAS framework, which requires non-null values, so you fill in missing responses with "I don't know." It then evaluates the generated answers based on answer correctness, context recall, and faithfulness.

The final step is to analyze the results to understand the system's performance.

8.2.6 Observations

You can review the overall summary in 8.5 to get an overview of the agent's performance.

Table 8.5 Benchmark summary

answer_correctness	context_recall	faithfulness
0.7774	0.7941	0.9657

The results in table 8.5 provide an overall assessment of the system's performance based on three key metrics. With an answer correctness score of 0.7774, the model gets things right most of the time but still misses the mark in about a quarter of cases. The context recall score of 0.7941 shows that while the retrieval system is doing a decent job, it occasionally fails to pull in all the necessary information, which could be holding back the overall accuracy. On the bright side, the faithfulness score of 0.9657 is excellent, meaning the model rarely makes things up and stays true to the retrieved context.

Overall, the high faithfulness score shows that the model does not introduce incorrect information, but the answer correctness and context recall lower scores suggest that improving retrieval mechanisms could lead to better response accuracy. Enhancing retrieval coverage and refining how the LLM formulates answers could improve overall performance. These insights can guide further optimizations, such as refining the retrieval system, improving query reformulation, or implementing better entity mapping for ambiguous queries.

You can further analyze each response to identify areas for improvement by using the code in the following listing.

Listing 8.4 Extracting metrics and adding them to the dataframe

```
for key in ["answer_correctness", "context_recall", "faithfulness"]:
    test_data[key] = [el[key] for el in result.scores]
test_data
```

The full response is too large to include in the book, but there are several key takeaways from analyzing individual examples. One noticeable pattern is that latency is significantly lower for queries that don't require text2cypher, as avoiding an additional LLM call speeds up the response. Another observation is that since we rely on an LLM as a judge, some scores may seem inconsistent, such as in the Hello example.

One clear limitation is that the system fails to answer the question "Who has the longest name among all actors?" This happens because the model isn't equipped to generate the appropriate Cypher query. To address this, you could add a few-shot example to guide text2cypher or implement a dedicated tool specifically for handling such queries.

This analysis demonstrates how a benchmark helps us evaluate results and make informed decisions about future improvements. As the system evolves, the benchmark dataset should continue to grow, ensuring ongoing refinement and better performance.

Throughout this book, you have explored how to build knowledge graph RAG systems. You've learned how different retrieval strategies enable your agent to fetch relevant information, whether from structured or unstructured data. Understanding when to use methods like vector search or Cypher templates is key to designing an efficient and accurate system.

By implementing and refining retrieval strategies, you now have the foundation to build a powerful knowledge graph–based agent. You've seen how structured queries can enhance precision and how retrieval choices impact answer quality, and you've learned how to systematically evaluate performance. This chapter introduced benchmarking as a way to measure accuracy, recall, and faithfulness, giving you the tools to continuously improve your agent.

8.3 Next steps

You're now equipped with the knowledge and tools to build and refine intelligent retrieval systems powered by knowledge graphs. Whether you're creating a sophisticated question-answering agent or tailoring retrieval pipelines for specific domains, you have the foundation to design robust, high-performing, knowledge-driven AI systems.

LLMs are rapidly improving, not only in their ability to understand and generate language but also in how effectively they can use external tools for data retrieval, transformation, and manipulation. As these models become more capable, they will be able to perform increasingly complex tasks with minimal prompting. However, their effectiveness still depends on the quality, design, and integration of the tools you provide. It's your job to implement those tools thoughtfully and efficiently, ensuring they are well suited to your system's goals and constraints.

With this foundation, you can now begin building your own agentic GraphRAG systems. You are equipped to work with unstructured data in a variety of ways: you can embed text directly to enable fast similarity-based retrieval or go a step further and extract structured information—such as entities, relationships, and events—to populate a knowledge graph that supports more precise, semantic, and multihop queries. By combining these approaches, you can build retrieval systems that not only find relevant information but truly understand it, paving the way for powerful, context-aware AI applications.

Summary

- Evaluating a RAG pipeline is crucial for ensuring accurate and coherent answers. A benchmark evaluation helps measure performance and define the agent's capabilities.
- The evaluation process involves assessing various stages: retrieval tool selection, context retrieval relevance, answer generation quality, and overall system effectiveness.
- A well-structured benchmark dataset should include diverse queries that test retrieval accuracy, entity mapping, the handling of greetings, irrelevant queries, and various Cypher-based database lookups.
- Instead of static expected answers, using Cypher queries as ground truth ensures the benchmark remains valid even if the underlying data changes.
- Context recall measures how well the system retrieves relevant information.
- Faithfulness evaluates if the generated answer is factually consistent with the retrieved content.
- Answer correctness assesses whether the response fully and accurately addresses the query.

appendix
The Neo4j environment

In this book, you will learn graph theory and algorithms through practical examples using Neo4j. I (Oskar) chose Neo4j because I have more than five years of experience with it, building and analyzing graphs.

Neo4j is a native graph database, built from the ground up to store, query, and manipulate graph data. It is implemented in Java and accessible from software written in other languages using the Cypher query language, through a transactional HTTP endpoint or the binary Bolt Protocol. In Neo4j, data is stored as nodes and relationships, which are both first-class citizens in the database. Nodes represent entities, such as people or businesses, and relationships represent the connections between these entities. Nodes and relationships can have properties, which are key–value pairs that provide additional information about the nodes and relationships.

Neo4j is designed to be highly scalable. It uses a flexible indexing system to efficiently query and manipulate data and supports atomicity, consistency, isolation, and durability transactions to ensure data consistency. It also has a built-in query language, called Cypher, which is designed to be expressive and easy to use for querying and manipulating graph data.

Another benefit of using Neo4j is that it has two useful plugins you will be using:

- *The Awesome Procedures on Cypher (APOC) plugin*—A library of procedures, functions, and plugins for Neo4j that provide a wide range of capabilities, including data import and export, data transformation and manipulation, date–time–interval processing, geospatial processing, text processing, and more.
- *The Graph Data Science (GDS) plugin*—A set of graph algorithms and procedures for Neo4j that allow users to perform advanced analytics on their graph data. GDS provides efficient, parallel implementations of common graph algorithms, such as shortest path, PageRank, and community detection. In addition, the plugin also includes node-embedding algorithms and machine learning workflows that support node classification and link prediction workflows.

A.1 Cypher query language

Cypher is a declarative query language for graph databases used to retrieve and manipulate data stored in a graph database. Cypher queries are written in a simple, human-readable syntax. The following listing is an example of a simple Cypher query that uses ASCII-art-style diagramming to illustrate the relationships being queried.

Listing A.1 A sample Cypher statement

```
MATCH (a:Person)-[:FOLLOWS]->(b:Person)
WHERE a.name = "Alice"
RETURN b.name
```

The openCypher initiative is a collaboration between Neo4j and several other organizations to promote the use of the Cypher query language as a standard for working with graph data. The goal of the initiative is to create a common language that can be used to query any graph database, regardless of the underlying technology. To achieve this goal, the openCypher initiative is making the Cypher language specification and related resources available under an open source license and is encouraging the development of Cypher implementations by a variety of organizations. So far, the Cypher query language has been adopted by Amazon, AgensGraph, Katana Graph, Memgraph, RedisGraph, and SAP HANA (openCypher Implementers Group, n.d.).

There is also an official ISO project to propose a unified graph query language (GQL) to interact with graph databases (GQL Standards Committee, n.d.). The GQL aims to build on the foundation of SQL and integrate proven ideas from existing graph query languages, including Cypher. That makes learning Cypher a great start to interact with graph databases, as it is already integrated with many of them and will also be part of the official ISO Graph Query Language. Take a look at the graph pattern matching proposal for GQL (Deutsch et al., 2022) for more information.

A.2 Neo4j installation

There are a few different options to set up your Neo4j environment:

- Neo4j Desktop
- Neo4j Docker
- Neo4j Aura

A.2.1 Neo4j Desktop installation

Neo4j Desktop is a local Neo4j graph database management application. It allows you to create database instances and install official plugins with only a few clicks. If you decide to use Neo4j Desktop, follow these steps to successfully start a Neo4j database instance with installed APOC and GDS plugins:

1. Download the Neo4j desktop application from the official website (https://neo4j.com/download; figure A.1).

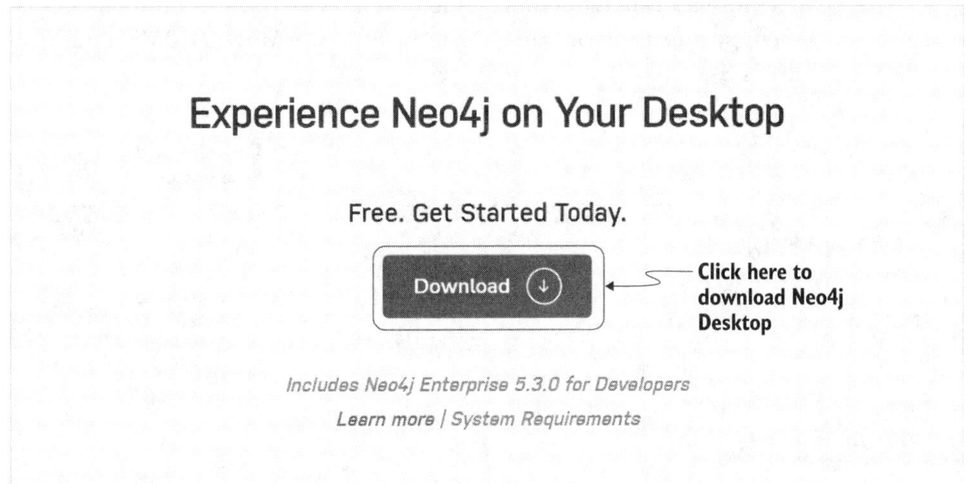

Figure A.1 Download Neo4j Desktop.

2 Install the Neo4j Desktop application on your computer and then open it.
3 Complete the registration step. You can enter the software key you were assigned when you downloaded the application or skip this step by clicking Register Later (figure A.2).

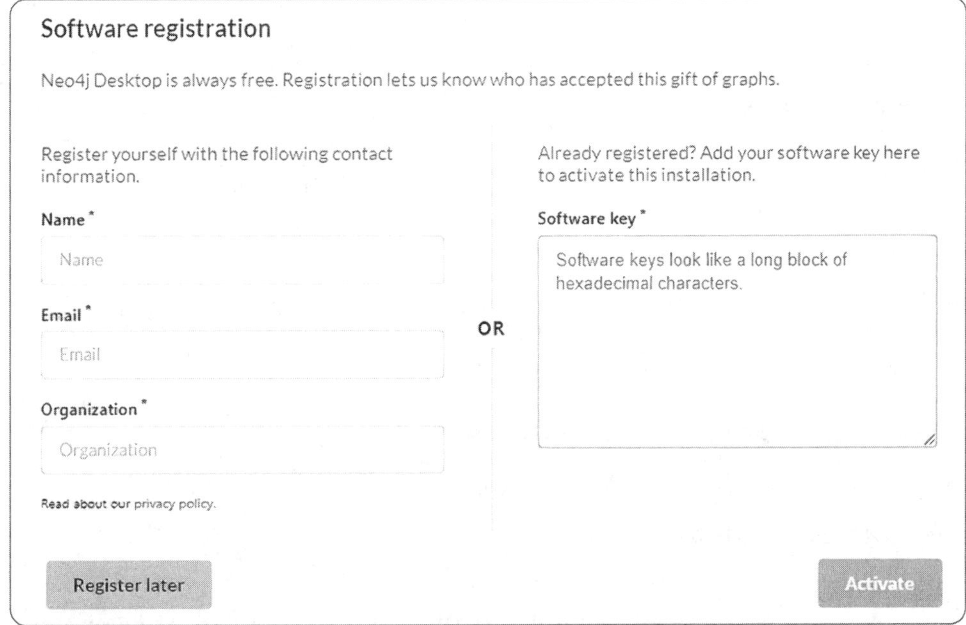

Figure A.2 Enter your personal information or skip the registration step.

4. The Movies Database Management System (DBMS) is automatically started on the first execution of Neo4j Desktop. Stop the Movies DBMS if it is running (figure A.3).

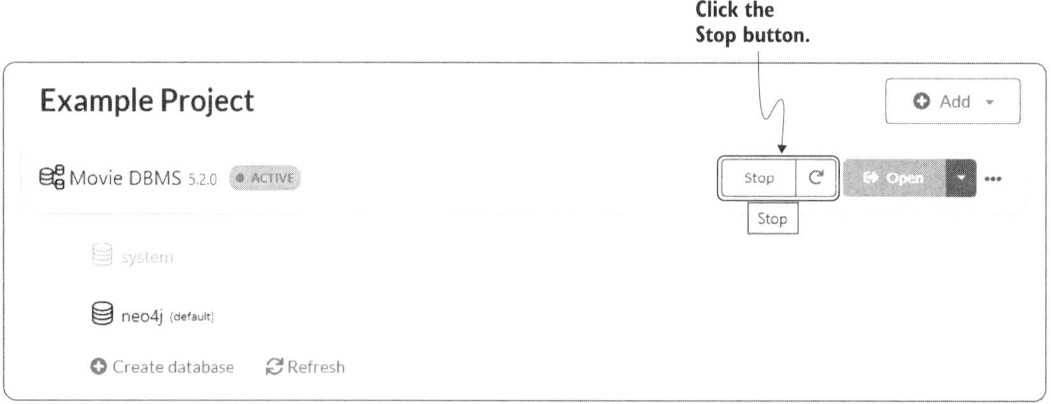

Figure A.3 Stop the default Movie DBMS database.

5. Add a new local DBMS (figure A.4).

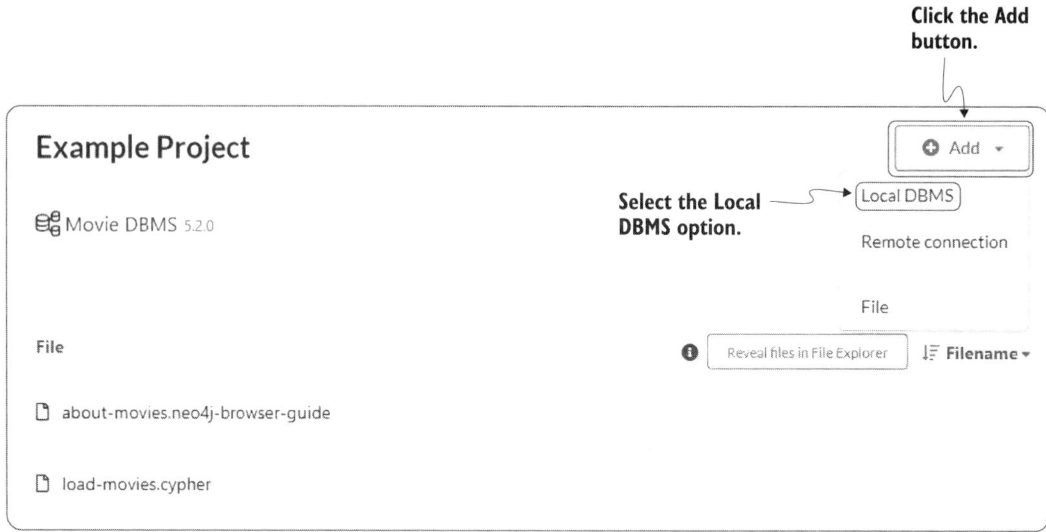

Figure A.4 Add a Local DBMS.

6. Type in any values for the DBMS name and password. Make sure to select version 5.9.0 or greater (figure A.5).

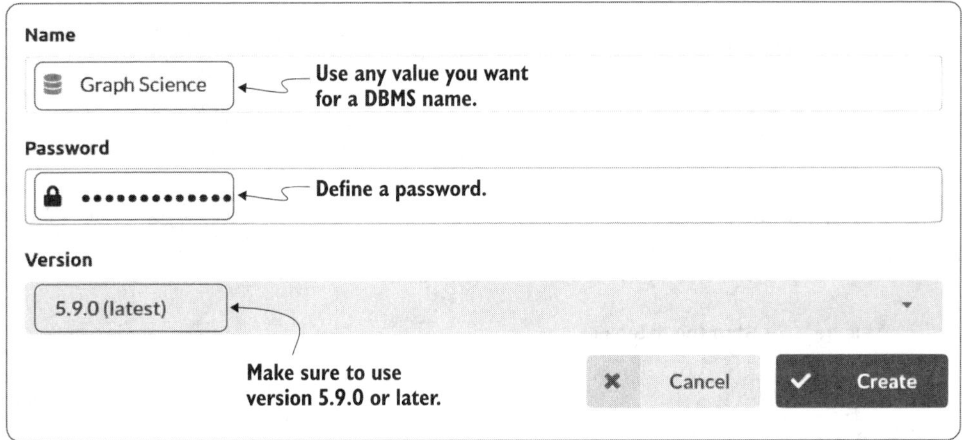

Figure A.5 Define a DBMS password and version.

7 Install APOC and GDS plugins by selecting the DBMS, which opens a right-hand pane with Details, Plugins, and Upgrade tabs. Select the Plugins tab, and then install the APOC and GDS plugins (figure A.6).

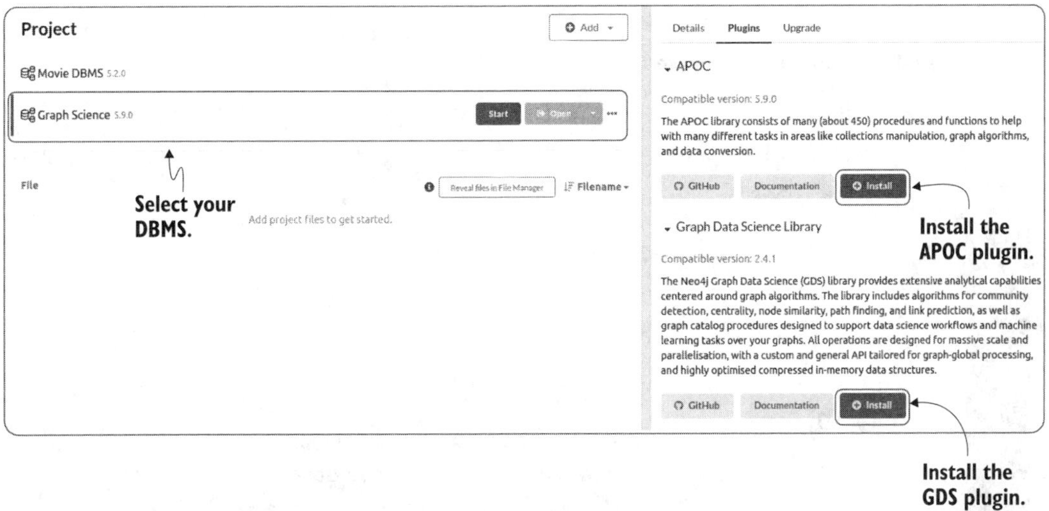

Figure A.6 Install the APOC and GDS plugins.

8 Start the database (figure A.7).
9 Open Neo4j Browser (figure A.8).
10 Execute Cypher queries by typing them in the Cypher editor. For longer Cypher statements, you can use the full-screen editor option (figure A.9).

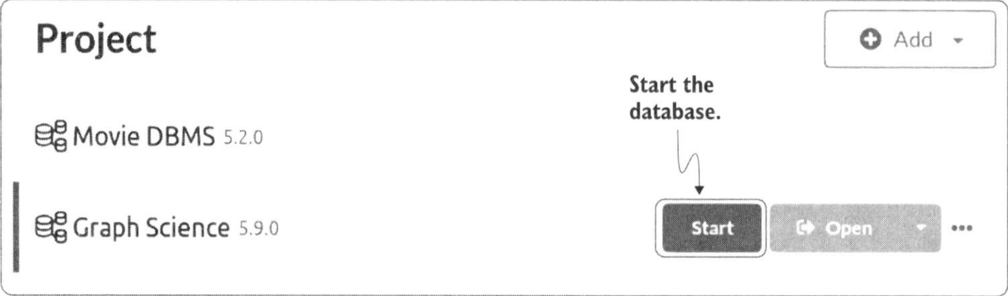

Figure A.7 Start the database.

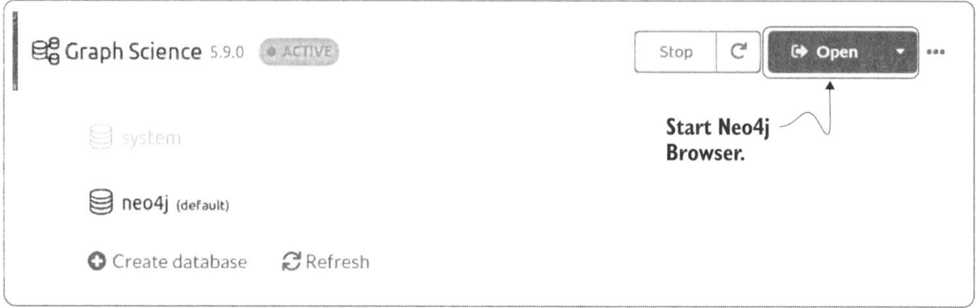

Figure A.8 Open Neo4j Browser.

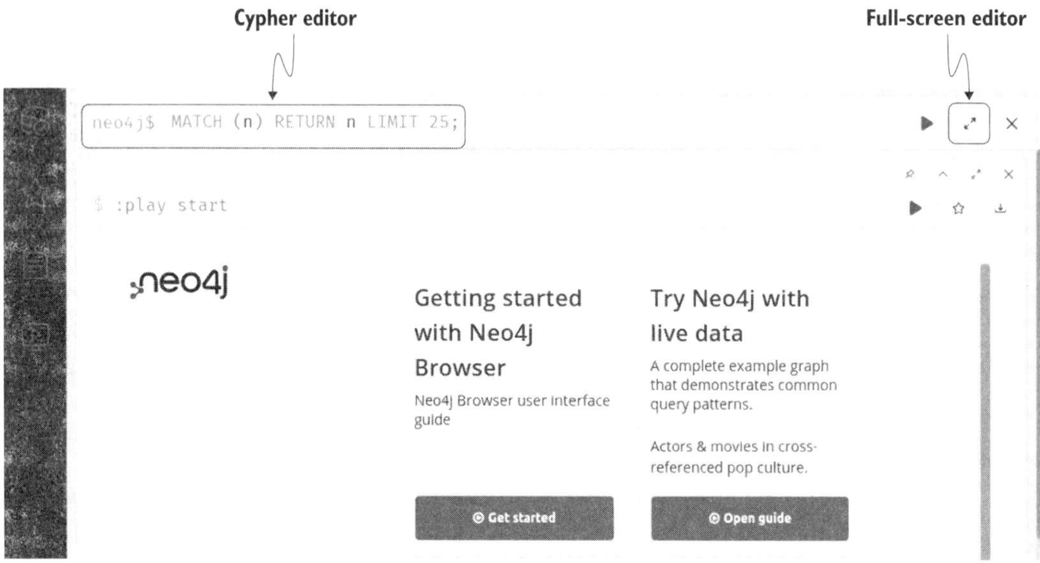

Figure A.9 The Cypher query editor in Neo4j Browser

A.2.2 Neo4j Docker installation

If you select the Neo4j Docker installation, you need to run the command in the following listing in your command prompt.

Listing A.2 Starting a Neo4j Docker

```
docker run \
  -p 7474:7474 -p 7687:7687 \
  -d \
  -v $HOME/neo4j/data:/data \
  -e NEO4J_AUTH=neo4j/password \
  -e 'NEO4J_PLUGINS=["apoc", "graph-data-science"]' \
    neo4j:5.26.0
```

This command starts a Dockerized Neo4j in the background. The APOC and GDS plugins are automatically added by defining the `NEO4J_PLUGINS` environment variable. It is a good practice to mount the `data` volume to persist the database files. The database username and password are specified with the `NEO4J_AUTH` variable.

Visit http://localhost:7474 in your web browser after you have executed the command in listing A.2. Type in the password, specified with the `NEO4J_AUTH` variable. The password in the example is `password`.

A.2.3 Neo4j Aura

Neo4j Aura is a hosted cloud instance of the Neo4j database. You can use it for all the chapters except for chapter 7, which requires GDS library. Unfortunately, the free version does not provide the GDS library. If you want to use the cloud-hosted Neo4j Aura to follow the examples in this book, you will need to use the AuraDS version, which provides support for GDS algorithms. You can find more information on Neo4j's official website: https://neo4j.com/product/auradb/.

A.3 Neo4j Browser configuration

Neo4j Browser has a beginner-friendly feature that visualizes all the relationships between resulting nodes, even when the relationships are not part of the query results. To avoid confusion, untick the Connect Result Nodes feature, as shown in figure A.10.

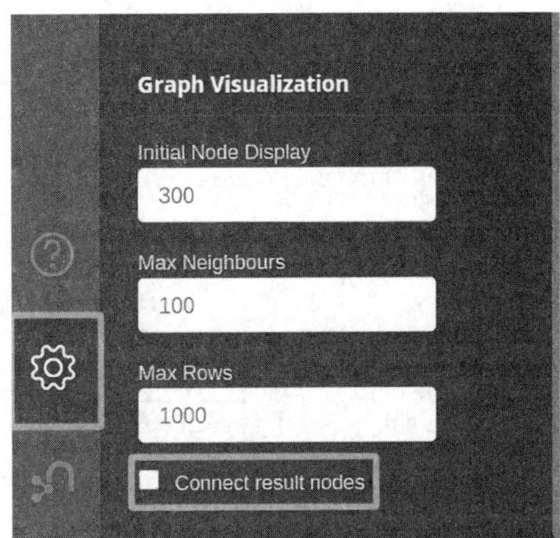

Figure A.10 Untick Connect Result Nodes in Neo4j Browser.

A.4 Movies dataset

In some chapters, we use the Movies dataset, which is a sample dataset that's small and easy to load. In the following, we provide the instructions on how to load the Movies dataset into your Neo4j instance.

A.4.1 Loading via the Neo4j Query Guide

When you're in Neo4j Query or Neo4j Browser, you can load the movies dataset by going through the "Movie Graph Guide" found in the guides sidebar or by executing `:play movies` in Neo4j Browser.

A.4.2 Trying the online version

There's also an online read-only version of this dataset available at https://demo.neo4jlabs.com:7473/browser/ (alternatively, using Bolt, https://demo.neo4jlabs.com:7687). The database name, username, and password are "movies."

A.4.3 Loading via Cypher

If you want to load the movies dataset directly using Cypher, use the query in the following listing.

Listing A.3 Loading the Movies dataset via Cypher

```
CREATE CONSTRAINT movie_title IF NOT EXISTS FOR (m:Movie)
REQUIRE m.title IS UNIQUE;
CREATE CONSTRAINT person_name IF NOT EXISTS FOR (p:Person)
REQUIRE p.name IS UNIQUE;

MERGE (TheMatrix:Movie {title:'The Matrix'}) ON CREATE SET
TheMatrix.released=1999, TheMatrix.tagline='Welcome to the Real World'

MERGE (Keanu:Person {name:'Keanu Reeves'}) ON CREATE SET Keanu.born=1964
MERGE (Carrie:Person {name:'Carrie-Anne Moss'})
ON CREATE SET Carrie.born=1967

MERGE (Laurence:Person {name:'Laurence Fishburne'})
ON CREATE SET Laurence.born=1961

MERGE (Hugo:Person {name:'Hugo Weaving'}) ON CREATE SET Hugo.born=1960
MERGE (LillyW:Person {name:'Lilly Wachowski'})
ON CREATE SET LillyW.born=1967
MERGE (LanaW:Person {name:'Lana Wachowski'}) ON CREATE SET LanaW.born=1965
MERGE (JoelS:Person {name:'Joel Silver'}) ON CREATE SET JoelS.born=1952

MERGE (Keanu)-[:ACTED_IN {roles:['Neo']}]->(TheMatrix)
MERGE (Carrie)-[:ACTED_IN {roles:['Trinity']}]->(TheMatrix)
MERGE (Laurence)-[:ACTED_IN {roles:['Morpheus']}]->(TheMatrix)
MERGE (Hugo)-[:ACTED_IN {roles:['Agent Smith']}]->(TheMatrix)
MERGE (LillyW)-[:DIRECTED]->(TheMatrix)
MERGE (LanaW)-[:DIRECTED]->(TheMatrix)
MERGE (JoelS)-[:PRODUCED]->(TheMatrix)
```

```
MERGE (Emil:Person {name:'Emil Eifrem'}) ON CREATE SET Emil.born=1978
MERGE (Emil)-[:ACTED_IN {roles:["Emil"]}]->(TheMatrix);


MERGE (TheMatrixReloaded:Movie {title:'The Matrix Reloaded'}) ON CREATE SET
TheMatrixReloaded.released=2003, TheMatrixReloaded.tagline='Free your mind'

MERGE (Keanu:Person {name:'Keanu Reeves'}) ON CREATE SET Keanu.born=1964
MERGE (Carrie:Person {name:'Carrie-Anne Moss'})
ON CREATE SET Carrie.born=1967

MERGE (Laurence:Person {name:'Laurence Fishburne'})
ON CREATE SET Laurence.born=1961

MERGE (Hugo:Person {name:'Hugo Weaving'}) ON CREATE SET Hugo.born=1960
MERGE (LillyW:Person {name:'Lilly Wachowski'})
ON CREATE SET LillyW.born=1967

MERGE (LanaW:Person {name:'Lana Wachowski'}) ON CREATE SET LanaW.born=1965
MERGE (JoelS:Person {name:'Joel Silver'}) ON CREATE SET JoelS.born=1952

MERGE (Keanu)-[:ACTED_IN {roles:['Neo']}]->(TheMatrixReloaded)
MERGE (Carrie)-[:ACTED_IN {roles:['Trinity']}]->(TheMatrixReloaded)
MERGE (Laurence)-[:ACTED_IN {roles:['Morpheus']}]->(TheMatrixReloaded)
MERGE (Hugo)-[:ACTED_IN {roles:['Agent Smith']}]->(TheMatrixReloaded)
MERGE (LillyW)-[:DIRECTED]->(TheMatrixReloaded)
MERGE (LanaW)-[:DIRECTED]->(TheMatrixReloaded)
MERGE (JoelS)-[:PRODUCED]->(TheMatrixReloaded);


MERGE (TheMatrixRevolutions:Movie {title:'The Matrix Revolutions'})
ON CREATE SET TheMatrixRevolutions.released=2003,
TheMatrixRevolutions.tagline='Everything that has a beginning has an end'

MERGE (Keanu:Person {name:'Keanu Reeves'}) ON CREATE SET Keanu.born=1964
MERGE (Carrie:Person {name:'Carrie-Anne Moss'})
ON CREATE SET Carrie.born=1967

MERGE (Laurence:Person {name:'Laurence Fishburne'})
ON CREATE SET Laurence.born=1961

MERGE (Hugo:Person {name:'Hugo Weaving'}) ON CREATE SET Hugo.born=1960
MERGE (LillyW:Person {name:'Lilly Wachowski'})
ON CREATE SET LillyW.born=1967

MERGE (LanaW:Person {name:'Lana Wachowski'}) ON CREATE SET LanaW.born=1965
MERGE (JoelS:Person {name:'Joel Silver'}) ON CREATE SET JoelS.born=1952

MERGE (Keanu)-[:ACTED_IN {roles:['Neo']}]->(TheMatrixRevolutions)
MERGE (Carrie)-[:ACTED_IN {roles:['Trinity']}]->(TheMatrixRevolutions)
MERGE (Laurence)-[:ACTED_IN {roles:['Morpheus']}]->(TheMatrixRevolutions)
MERGE (Hugo)-[:ACTED_IN {roles:['Agent Smith']}]->(TheMatrixRevolutions)
```

```
MERGE (LillyW)-[:DIRECTED]->(TheMatrixRevolutions)
MERGE (LanaW)-[:DIRECTED]->(TheMatrixRevolutions)
MERGE (JoelS)-[:PRODUCED]->(TheMatrixRevolutions);


MERGE (TheDevilsAdvocate:Movie
{
  title:"The Devil's Advocate",
  released:1997,
  tagline:'Evil has its winning ways'
})

MERGE (Keanu:Person {name:'Keanu Reeves'}) ON CREATE SET Keanu.born=1964
MERGE (Charlize:Person {name:'Charlize Theron'})
ON CREATE SET Charlize.born=1975
MERGE (Al:Person {name:'Al Pacino'}) ON CREATE SET Al.born=1940
MERGE (Taylor:Person {name:'Taylor Hackford'})
ON CREATE SET Taylor.born=1944

MERGE (Keanu)-[:ACTED_IN {roles:['Kevin Lomax']}]->(TheDevilsAdvocate)
MERGE (Charlize)-[:ACTED_IN {roles:['Mary Ann Lomax']}]->(TheDevilsAdvocate)
MERGE (Al)-[:ACTED_IN {roles:['John Milton']}]->(TheDevilsAdvocate)
MERGE (Taylor)-[:DIRECTED]->(TheDevilsAdvocate);


MERGE (AFewGoodMen:Movie {title:'A Few Good Men'})
ON CREATE SET
AFewGoodMen.released=1992,
AFewGoodMen.tagline='In the heart of the nation\'s capital,
➥ in a courthouse of the U.S. government, one man will stop at nothing to
➥ keep his honor, and one will stop at nothing to find the truth.'

MERGE (TomC:Person {name:'Tom Cruise'}) ON CREATE SET TomC.born=1962
MERGE (JackN:Person {name:'Jack Nicholson'}) ON CREATE SET JackN.born=1937
MERGE (DemiM:Person {name:'Demi Moore'}) ON CREATE SET DemiM.born=1962
MERGE (KevinB:Person {name:'Kevin Bacon'}) ON CREATE SET KevinB.born=1958
MERGE (KieferS:Person {name:'Kiefer Sutherland'})
ON CREATE SET KieferS.born=1966

MERGE (NoahW:Person {name:'Noah Wyle'}) ON CREATE SET NoahW.born=1971
MERGE (CubaG:Person {name:'Cuba Gooding Jr.'}) ON CREATE SET CubaG.born=1968
MERGE (KevinP:Person {name:'Kevin Pollak'}) ON CREATE SET KevinP.born=1957
MERGE (JTW:Person {name:'J.T. Walsh'}) ON CREATE SET JTW.born=1943
MERGE (JamesM:Person {name:'James Marshall'}) ON CREATE SET JamesM.born=1967
MERGE (ChristopherG:Person {name:'Christopher Guest'})
ON CREATE SET ChristopherG.born=1948

MERGE (RobR:Person {name:'Rob Reiner'}) ON CREATE SET RobR.born=1947
MERGE (AaronS:Person {name:'Aaron Sorkin'}) ON CREATE SET AaronS.born=1961

MERGE (TomC)-[:ACTED_IN {roles:['Lt. Daniel Kaffee']}]->(AFewGoodMen)
MERGE (JackN)-[:ACTED_IN {roles:['Col. Nathan R. Jessup']}]->(AFewGoodMen)
```

```
MERGE (DemiM)-[:ACTED_IN {
  roles:['Lt. Cdr. JoAnne Galloway']
}]->(AFewGoodMen)

MERGE (KevinB)-[:ACTED_IN {
  roles:['Capt. Jack Ross']
}]->(AFewGoodMen)
MERGE (KieferS)-[:ACTED_IN {roles:['Lt. Jonathan Kendrick']}]->(AFewGoodMen)
MERGE (NoahW)-[:ACTED_IN {roles:['Cpl. Jeffrey Barnes']}]->(AFewGoodMen)
MERGE (CubaG)-[:ACTED_IN {roles:['Cpl. Carl Hammaker']}]->(AFewGoodMen)
MERGE (KevinP)-[:ACTED_IN {roles:['Lt. Sam Weinberg']}]->(AFewGoodMen)
MERGE (JTW)-[:ACTED_IN {
  roles:['Lt. Col. Matthew Andrew Markinson']
}]->(AFewGoodMen)

MERGE (JamesM)-[:ACTED_IN {roles:['Pfc. Louden Downey']}]->(AFewGoodMen)
MERGE (ChristopherG)-[:ACTED_IN {roles:['Dr. Stone']}]->(AFewGoodMen)
MERGE (AaronS)-[:ACTED_IN {roles:['Man in Bar']}]->(AFewGoodMen)
MERGE (RobR)-[:DIRECTED]->(AFewGoodMen)
MERGE (AaronS)-[:WROTE]->(AFewGoodMen);


MERGE (TopGun:Movie {title:'Top Gun'}) ON CREATE SET
TopGun.released=1986, TopGun.tagline='I feel the need, the need for speed.'

MERGE (TomC:Person {name:'Tom Cruise'}) ON CREATE SET TomC.born=1962
MERGE (KellyM:Person {name:'Kelly McGillis'}) ON CREATE SET KellyM.born=1957
MERGE (ValK:Person {name:'Val Kilmer'}) ON CREATE SET ValK.born=1959
MERGE (AnthonyE:Person {name:'Anthony Edwards'})
ON CREATE SET AnthonyE.born=1962

MERGE (TomS:Person {name:'Tom Skerritt'}) ON CREATE SET TomS.born=1933
MERGE (MegR:Person {name:'Meg Ryan'}) ON CREATE SET MegR.born=1961
MERGE (TonyS:Person {name:'Tony Scott'}) ON CREATE SET TonyS.born=1944
MERGE (JimC:Person {name:'Jim Cash'}) ON CREATE SET JimC.born=1941

MERGE (TomC)-[:ACTED_IN {roles:['Maverick']}]->(TopGun)
MERGE (KellyM)-[:ACTED_IN {roles:['Charlie']}]->(TopGun)
MERGE (ValK)-[:ACTED_IN {roles:['Iceman']}]->(TopGun)
MERGE (AnthonyE)-[:ACTED_IN {roles:['Goose']}]->(TopGun)
MERGE (TomS)-[:ACTED_IN {roles:['Viper']}]->(TopGun)
MERGE (MegR)-[:ACTED_IN {roles:['Carole']}]->(TopGun)
MERGE (TonyS)-[:DIRECTED]->(TopGun)
MERGE (JimC)-[:WROTE]->(TopGun);


MERGE (JerryMaguire:Movie {title:'Jerry Maguire'}) ON CREATE SET
JerryMaguire.released=2000,
JerryMaguire.tagline='The rest of his life begins now.'

MERGE (TomC:Person {name:'Tom Cruise'}) ON CREATE SET TomC.born=1962
MERGE (CubaG:Person {name:'Cuba Gooding Jr.'}) ON CREATE SET CubaG.born=1968
MERGE (ReneeZ:Person {name:'Renee Zellweger'})
ON CREATE SET ReneeZ.born=1969
MERGE (KellyP:Person {name:'Kelly Preston'}) ON CREATE SET KellyP.born=1962
```

```
MERGE (JerryO:Person {name:'Jerry O\'Connell'})
ON CREATE SET JerryO.born=1974
MERGE (JayM:Person {name:'Jay Mohr'}) ON CREATE SET JayM.born=1970
MERGE (BonnieH:Person {name:'Bonnie Hunt'}) ON CREATE SET BonnieH.born=1961
MERGE (ReginaK:Person {name:'Regina King'}) ON CREATE SET ReginaK.born=1971
MERGE (JonathanL:Person {name:'Jonathan Lipnicki'})
ON CREATE SET JonathanL.born=1996
MERGE (CameronC:Person {name:'Cameron Crowe'})
ON CREATE SET CameronC.born=1957

MERGE (TomC)-[:ACTED_IN {roles:['Jerry Maguire']}]->(JerryMaguire)
MERGE (CubaG)-[:ACTED_IN {roles:['Rod Tidwell']}]->(JerryMaguire)
MERGE (ReneeZ)-[:ACTED_IN {roles:['Dorothy Boyd']}]->(JerryMaguire)
MERGE (KellyP)-[:ACTED_IN {roles:['Avery Bishop']}]->(JerryMaguire)
MERGE (JerryO)-[:ACTED_IN {roles:['Frank Cushman']}]->(JerryMaguire)
MERGE (JayM)-[:ACTED_IN {roles:['Bob Sugar']}]->(JerryMaguire)
MERGE (BonnieH)-[:ACTED_IN {roles:['Laurel Boyd']}]->(JerryMaguire)
MERGE (ReginaK)-[:ACTED_IN {roles:['Marcee Tidwell']}]->(JerryMaguire)
MERGE (JonathanL)-[:ACTED_IN {roles:['Ray Boyd']}]->(JerryMaguire)
MERGE (CameronC)-[:DIRECTED]->(JerryMaguire)
MERGE (CameronC)-[:PRODUCED]->(JerryMaguire)
MERGE (CameronC)-[:WROTE]->(JerryMaguire);

MERGE (StandByMe:Movie {title:'Stand By Me'})
ON CREATE SET StandByMe.released=1986,
StandByMe.tagline='For some, it\'s the last real taste of innocence, and
➥ the first real taste of life. But for everyone, it\'s the time that
➥ memories are made of.'

MERGE (RiverP:Person {name:'River Phoenix'}) ON CREATE SET RiverP.born=1970
MERGE (CoreyF:Person {name:'Corey Feldman'}) ON CREATE SET CoreyF.born=1971
MERGE (JerryO:Person {name:'Jerry O\'Connell'})
ON CREATE SET JerryO.born=1974
MERGE (WilW:Person {name:'Wil Wheaton'}) ON CREATE SET WilW.born=1972
MERGE (KieferS:Person {name:'Kiefer Sutherland'})
ON CREATE SET KieferS.born=1966
MERGE (JohnC:Person {name:'John Cusack'}) ON CREATE SET JohnC.born=1966
MERGE (MarshallB:Person {name:'Marshall Bell'})
ON CREATE SET MarshallB.born=1942
MERGE (RobR:Person {name:'Rob Reiner'}) ON CREATE SET RobR.born=1947

MERGE (WilW)-[:ACTED_IN {roles:['Gordie Lachance']}]->(StandByMe)
MERGE (RiverP)-[:ACTED_IN {roles:['Chris Chambers']}]->(StandByMe)
MERGE (JerryO)-[:ACTED_IN {roles:['Vern Tessio']}]->(StandByMe)
MERGE (CoreyF)-[:ACTED_IN {roles:['Teddy Duchamp']}]->(StandByMe)
MERGE (JohnC)-[:ACTED_IN {roles:['Denny Lachance']}]->(StandByMe)
MERGE (KieferS)-[:ACTED_IN {roles:['Ace Merrill']}]->(StandByMe)
MERGE (MarshallB)-[:ACTED_IN {roles:['Mr. Lachance']}]->(StandByMe)
MERGE (RobR)-[:DIRECTED]->(StandByMe);

MERGE (AsGoodAsItGets:Movie {title:'As Good as It Gets'})
ON CREATE SET AsGoodAsItGets.released=1997,
AsGoodAsItGets.tagline='A comedy from the heart that goes for the throat.'
```

```
MERGE (JackN:Person {name:'Jack Nicholson'}) ON CREATE SET JackN.born=1937
MERGE (HelenH:Person {name:'Helen Hunt'}) ON CREATE SET HelenH.born=1963
MERGE (GregK:Person {name:'Greg Kinnear'}) ON CREATE SET GregK.born=1963
MERGE (JamesB:Person {name:'James L. Brooks'})
ON CREATE SET JamesB.born=1940
MERGE (CubaG:Person {name:'Cuba Gooding Jr.'}) ON CREATE SET CubaG.born=1968

MERGE (JackN)-[:ACTED_IN {roles:['Melvin Udall']}]->(AsGoodAsItGets)
MERGE (HelenH)-[:ACTED_IN {roles:['Carol Connelly']}]->(AsGoodAsItGets)
MERGE (GregK)-[:ACTED_IN {roles:['Simon Bishop']}]->(AsGoodAsItGets)
MERGE (CubaG)-[:ACTED_IN {roles:['Frank Sachs']}]->(AsGoodAsItGets)
MERGE (JamesB)-[:DIRECTED]->(AsGoodAsItGets);

MERGE (WhatDreamsMayCome:Movie {title:'What Dreams May Come'})
ON CREATE SET WhatDreamsMayCome.released=1998,
WhatDreamsMayCome.tagline='After life there is more. The end is just the
➥ beginning.'

MERGE (AnnabellaS:Person {name:'Annabella Sciorra'})
ON CREATE SET AnnabellaS.born=1960
MERGE (MaxS:Person {name:'Max von Sydow'}) ON CREATE SET MaxS.born=1929
MERGE (WernerH:Person {name:'Werner Herzog'})
ON CREATE SET WernerH.born=1942
MERGE (Robin:Person {name:'Robin Williams'}) ON CREATE SET Robin.born=1951
MERGE (VincentW:Person {name:'Vincent Ward'})
ON CREATE SET VincentW.born=1956
MERGE (CubaG:Person {name:'Cuba Gooding Jr.'}) ON CREATE SET CubaG.born=1968

MERGE (Robin)-[:ACTED_IN {roles:['Chris Nielsen']}]->(WhatDreamsMayCome)
MERGE (CubaG)-[:ACTED_IN {roles:['Albert Lewis']}]->(WhatDreamsMayCome)
MERGE (AnnabellaS)-[:ACTED_IN {
  roles:['Annie Collins-Nielsen']
}]->(WhatDreamsMayCome)
MERGE (MaxS)-[:ACTED_IN {roles:['The Tracker']}]->(WhatDreamsMayCome)
MERGE (WernerH)-[:ACTED_IN {roles:['The Face']}]->(WhatDreamsMayCome)
MERGE (VincentW)-[:DIRECTED]->(WhatDreamsMayCome);

MERGE (SnowFallingonCedars:Movie {title:'Snow Falling on Cedars'})
ON CREATE SET SnowFallingonCedars.released=1999,
SnowFallingonCedars.tagline='First loves last. Forever.'

MERGE (EthanH:Person {name:'Ethan Hawke'}) ON CREATE SET EthanH.born=1970
MERGE (RickY:Person {name:'Rick Yune'}) ON CREATE SET RickY.born=1971
MERGE (JamesC:Person {name:'James Cromwell'}) ON CREATE SET JamesC.born=1940
MERGE (ScottH:Person {name:'Scott Hicks'}) ON CREATE SET ScottH.born=1953
MERGE (MaxS:Person {name:'Max von Sydow'}) ON CREATE SET MaxS.born=1929

MERGE (EthanH)-[:ACTED_IN {
  roles:['Ishmael Chambers']
}]->(SnowFallingonCedars)
MERGE (RickY)-[:ACTED_IN {roles:['Kazuo Miyamoto']}]->(SnowFallingonCedars)
MERGE (MaxS)-[:ACTED_IN {roles:['Nels Gudmundsson']}]->(SnowFallingonCedars)
MERGE (JamesC)-[:ACTED_IN {roles:['Judge Fielding']}]->(SnowFallingonCedars)
MERGE (ScottH)-[:DIRECTED]->(SnowFallingonCedars);
```

```
MERGE (YouveGotMail:Movie {title:'You\'ve Got Mail'}) ON CREATE SET
YouveGotMail.released=1998,
YouveGotMail.tagline='At odds in life... in love on-line.'

MERGE (TomH:Person {name:'Tom Hanks'}) ON CREATE SET TomH.born=1956
MERGE (MegR:Person {name:'Meg Ryan'}) ON CREATE SET MegR.born=1961
MERGE (GregK:Person {name:'Greg Kinnear'}) ON CREATE SET GregK.born=1963
MERGE (ParkerP:Person {name:'Parker Posey'}) ON CREATE SET ParkerP.born=1968
MERGE (DaveC:Person {name:'Dave Chappelle'}) ON CREATE SET DaveC.born=1973
MERGE (SteveZ:Person {name:'Steve Zahn'}) ON CREATE SET SteveZ.born=1967
MERGE (NoraE:Person {name:'Nora Ephron'}) ON CREATE SET NoraE.born=1941

MERGE (TomH)-[:ACTED_IN {roles:['Joe Fox']}]->(YouveGotMail)
MERGE (MegR)-[:ACTED_IN {roles:['Kathleen Kelly']}]->(YouveGotMail)
MERGE (GregK)-[:ACTED_IN {roles:['Frank Navasky']}]->(YouveGotMail)
MERGE (ParkerP)-[:ACTED_IN {roles:['Patricia Eden']}]->(YouveGotMail)
MERGE (DaveC)-[:ACTED_IN {roles:['Kevin Jackson']}]->(YouveGotMail)
MERGE (SteveZ)-[:ACTED_IN {roles:['George Pappas']}]->(YouveGotMail)
MERGE (NoraE)-[:DIRECTED]->(YouveGotMail);

MERGE (SleeplessInSeattle:Movie {title:'Sleepless in Seattle'})
ON CREATE SET SleeplessInSeattle.released=1993,
SleeplessInSeattle.tagline='What if someone you never met, someone you never
➥ saw, someone you never knew was the only someone for you?'

MERGE (TomH:Person {name:'Tom Hanks'}) ON CREATE SET TomH.born=1956
MERGE (MegR:Person {name:'Meg Ryan'}) ON CREATE SET MegR.born=1961
MERGE (RitaW:Person {name:'Rita Wilson'}) ON CREATE SET RitaW.born=1956
MERGE (BillPull:Person {name:'Bill Pullman'})
ON CREATE SET BillPull.born=1953
MERGE (VictorG:Person {name:'Victor Garber'})
ON CREATE SET VictorG.born=1949
MERGE (RosieO:Person {name:'Rosie O\'Donnell'})
ON CREATE SET RosieO.born=1962
MERGE (NoraE:Person {name:'Nora Ephron'}) ON CREATE SET NoraE.born=1941

MERGE (TomH)-[:ACTED_IN {roles:['Sam Baldwin']}]->(SleeplessInSeattle)
MERGE (MegR)-[:ACTED_IN {roles:['Annie Reed']}]->(SleeplessInSeattle)
MERGE (RitaW)-[:ACTED_IN {roles:['Suzy']}]->(SleeplessInSeattle)
MERGE (BillPull)-[:ACTED_IN {roles:['Walter']}]->(SleeplessInSeattle)
MERGE (VictorG)-[:ACTED_IN {roles:['Greg']}]->(SleeplessInSeattle)
MERGE (RosieO)-[:ACTED_IN {roles:['Becky']}]->(SleeplessInSeattle)
MERGE (NoraE)-[:DIRECTED]->(SleeplessInSeattle);

MERGE (JoeVersustheVolcano:Movie {title:'Joe Versus the Volcano'})
ON CREATE SET JoeVersustheVolcano.released=1990,
JoeVersustheVolcano.tagline='A story of love, lava and burning desire.'

MERGE (TomH:Person {name:'Tom Hanks'}) ON CREATE SET TomH.born=1956
MERGE (MegR:Person {name:'Meg Ryan'}) ON CREATE SET MegR.born=1961
MERGE (JohnS:Person {name:'John Patrick Stanley'})
ON CREATE SET JohnS.born=1950
MERGE (Nathan:Person {name:'Nathan Lane'}) ON CREATE SET Nathan.born=1956
```

```
MERGE (TomH)-[:ACTED_IN {roles:['Joe Banks']}]->(JoeVersustheVolcano)
MERGE (MegR)-[:ACTED_IN {
  roles:['DeDe', 'Angelica Graynamore', 'Patricia Graynamore']
}]->(JoeVersustheVolcano)
MERGE (Nathan)-[:ACTED_IN {roles:['Baw']}]->(JoeVersustheVolcano)
MERGE (JohnS)-[:DIRECTED]->(JoeVersustheVolcano);

MERGE (WhenHarryMetSally:Movie {title:'When Harry Met Sally'}) ON CREATE SET
 WhenHarryMetSally.released=1998,
 WhenHarryMetSally.tagline='Can two friends sleep together and still love
 ➥ each other in the morning?'

MERGE (MegR:Person {name:'Meg Ryan'}) ON CREATE SET MegR.born=1961
MERGE (BillyC:Person {name:'Billy Crystal'}) ON CREATE SET BillyC.born=1948
MERGE (CarrieF:Person {name:'Carrie Fisher'})
ON CREATE SET CarrieF.born=1956
MERGE (BrunoK:Person {name:'Bruno Kirby'}) ON CREATE SET BrunoK.born=1949
MERGE (RobR:Person {name:'Rob Reiner'}) ON CREATE SET RobR.born=1947
MERGE (NoraE:Person {name:'Nora Ephron'}) ON CREATE SET NoraE.born=1941

MERGE (BillyC)-[:ACTED_IN {roles:['Harry Burns']}]->(WhenHarryMetSally)
MERGE (MegR)-[:ACTED_IN {roles:['Sally Albright']}]->(WhenHarryMetSally)
MERGE (CarrieF)-[:ACTED_IN {roles:['Marie']}]->(WhenHarryMetSally)
MERGE (BrunoK)-[:ACTED_IN {roles:['Jess']}]->(WhenHarryMetSally)
MERGE (RobR)-[:DIRECTED]->(WhenHarryMetSally)
MERGE (RobR)-[:PRODUCED]->(WhenHarryMetSally)
MERGE (NoraE)-[:PRODUCED]->(WhenHarryMetSally)
MERGE (NoraE)-[:WROTE]->(WhenHarryMetSally);

MERGE (ThatThingYouDo:Movie {title:'That Thing You Do'})
ON CREATE SET ThatThingYouDo.released=1996,
ThatThingYouDo.tagline='In every life there comes a time when that thing you
➥ dream becomes that thing you do'

MERGE (TomH:Person {name:'Tom Hanks'}) ON CREATE SET TomH.born=1956
MERGE (LivT:Person {name:'Liv Tyler'}) ON CREATE SET LivT.born=1977
MERGE (Charlize:Person {name:'Charlize Theron'})
ON CREATE SET Charlize.born=1975

MERGE (TomH)-[:ACTED_IN {roles:['Mr. White']}]->(ThatThingYouDo)
MERGE (LivT)-[:ACTED_IN {roles:['Faye Dolan']}]->(ThatThingYouDo)
MERGE (Charlize)-[:ACTED_IN {roles:['Tina']}]->(ThatThingYouDo)
MERGE (TomH)-[:DIRECTED]->(ThatThingYouDo);

MERGE (TheReplacements:Movie {title:'The Replacements'}) ON CREATE SET
TheReplacements.released=2000,
TheReplacements.tagline='Pain heals, Chicks dig scars... Glory lasts forever'

MERGE (Keanu:Person {name:'Keanu Reeves'}) ON CREATE SET Keanu.born=1964
MERGE (Brooke:Person {name:'Brooke Langton'}) ON CREATE SET Brooke.born=1970
MERGE (Gene:Person {name:'Gene Hackman'}) ON CREATE SET Gene.born=1930
MERGE (Orlando:Person {name:'Orlando Jones'})
ON CREATE SET Orlando.born=1968
MERGE (Howard:Person {name:'Howard Deutch'}) ON CREATE SET Howard.born=1950
```

```
MERGE (Keanu)-[:ACTED_IN {roles:['Shane Falco']}]->(TheReplacements)
MERGE (Brooke)-[:ACTED_IN {roles:['Annabelle Farrell']}]->(TheReplacements)
MERGE (Gene)-[:ACTED_IN {roles:['Jimmy McGinty']}]->(TheReplacements)
MERGE (Orlando)-[:ACTED_IN {roles:['Clifford Franklin']}]->(TheReplacements)
MERGE (Howard)-[:DIRECTED]->(TheReplacements);

MERGE (RescueDawn:Movie {title:'RescueDawn'}) ON CREATE SET
RescueDawn.released=2006,
RescueDawn.tagline='Based on the extraordinary true story of one man\'s
➥ fight for freedom'

MERGE (ChristianB:Person {name:'Christian Bale'})
ON CREATE SET ChristianB.born=1974
MERGE (ZachG:Person {name:'Zach Grenier'}) ON CREATE SET ZachG.born=1954
MERGE (MarshallB:Person {name:'Marshall Bell'})
ON CREATE SET MarshallB.born=1942
MERGE (SteveZ:Person {name:'Steve Zahn'}) ON CREATE SET SteveZ.born=1967
MERGE (WernerH:Person {name:'Werner Herzog'})
ON CREATE SET WernerH.born=1942

MERGE (MarshallB)-[:ACTED_IN {roles:['Admiral']}]->(RescueDawn)
MERGE (ChristianB)-[:ACTED_IN {roles:['Dieter Dengler']}]->(RescueDawn)
MERGE (ZachG)-[:ACTED_IN {roles:['Squad Leader']}]->(RescueDawn)
MERGE (SteveZ)-[:ACTED_IN {roles:['Duane']}]->(RescueDawn)
MERGE (WernerH)-[:DIRECTED]->(RescueDawn);

MERGE (TheBirdcage:Movie {title:'The Birdcage'}) ON CREATE SET
TheBirdcage.released=1996, TheBirdcage.tagline='Come as you are'

MERGE (MikeN:Person {name:'Mike Nichols'}) ON CREATE SET MikeN.born=1931
MERGE (Robin:Person {name:'Robin Williams'}) ON CREATE SET Robin.born=1951
MERGE (Nathan:Person {name:'Nathan Lane'}) ON CREATE SET Nathan.born=1956
MERGE (Gene:Person {name:'Gene Hackman'}) ON CREATE SET Gene.born=1930

MERGE (Robin)-[:ACTED_IN {roles:['Armand Goldman']}]->(TheBirdcage)
MERGE (Nathan)-[:ACTED_IN {roles:['Albert Goldman']}]->(TheBirdcage)
MERGE (Gene)-[:ACTED_IN {roles:['Sen. Kevin Keeley']}]->(TheBirdcage)
MERGE (MikeN)-[:DIRECTED]->(TheBirdcage);

MERGE (Unforgiven:Movie {title:'Unforgiven'}) ON CREATE SET
Unforgiven.released=1992,
Unforgiven.tagline='It\'s a hell of a thing, killing a man'

MERGE (Gene:Person {name:'Gene Hackman'}) ON CREATE SET Gene.born=1930
MERGE (RichardH:Person {name:'Richard Harris'})
ON CREATE SET RichardH.born=1930
MERGE (ClintE:Person {name:'Clint Eastwood'}) ON CREATE SET ClintE.born=1930

MERGE (RichardH)-[:ACTED_IN {roles:['English Bob']}]->(Unforgiven)
MERGE (ClintE)-[:ACTED_IN {roles:['Bill Munny']}]->(Unforgiven)
MERGE (Gene)-[:ACTED_IN {roles:['Little Bill Daggett']}]->(Unforgiven)
MERGE (ClintE)-[:DIRECTED]->(Unforgiven);

MERGE (JohnnyMnemonic:Movie {title:'Johnny Mnemonic'}) ON CREATE SET
JohnnyMnemonic.released=1995,
```

```
JohnnyMnemonic.tagline='The hottest data on earth. In the coolest head in
➥ town'

MERGE (Keanu:Person {name:'Keanu Reeves'}) ON CREATE SET Keanu.born=1964
MERGE (Takeshi:Person {name:'Takeshi Kitano'})
ON CREATE SET Takeshi.born=1947
MERGE (Dina:Person {name:'Dina Meyer'}) ON CREATE SET Dina.born=1968
MERGE (IceT:Person {name:'Ice-T'}) ON CREATE SET IceT.born=1958
MERGE (RobertL:Person {name:'Robert Longo'}) ON CREATE SET RobertL.born=1953

MERGE (Keanu)-[:ACTED_IN {roles:['Johnny Mnemonic']}]->(JohnnyMnemonic)
MERGE (Takeshi)-[:ACTED_IN {roles:['Takahashi']}]->(JohnnyMnemonic)
MERGE (Dina)-[:ACTED_IN {roles:['Jane']}]->(JohnnyMnemonic)
MERGE (IceT)-[:ACTED_IN {roles:['J-Bone']}]->(JohnnyMnemonic)
MERGE (RobertL)-[:DIRECTED]->(JohnnyMnemonic);

MERGE (CloudAtlas:Movie {title:'Cloud Atlas'}) ON CREATE SET
CloudAtlas.released=2012, CloudAtlas.tagline='Everything is connected'

MERGE (TomH:Person {name:'Tom Hanks'}) ON CREATE SET TomH.born=1956
MERGE (Hugo:Person {name:'Hugo Weaving'}) ON CREATE SET Hugo.born=1960
MERGE (HalleB:Person {name:'Halle Berry'}) ON CREATE SET HalleB.born=1966
MERGE (JimB:Person {name:'Jim Broadbent'}) ON CREATE SET JimB.born=1949
MERGE (TomT:Person {name:'Tom Tykwer'}) ON CREATE SET TomT.born=1965
MERGE (DavidMitchell:Person {name:'David Mitchell'})
ON CREATE SET DavidMitchell.born=1969
MERGE (StefanArndt:Person {name:'Stefan Arndt'})
ON CREATE SET StefanArndt.born=1961
MERGE (LillyW:Person {name:'Lilly Wachowski'})
ON CREATE SET LillyW.born=1967
MERGE (LanaW:Person {name:'Lana Wachowski'}) ON CREATE SET LanaW.born=1965

MERGE (TomH)-[:ACTED_IN {
  roles:['Zachry', 'Dr. Henry Goose', 'Isaac Sachs', 'Dermot Hoggins']
}]->(CloudAtlas)
MERGE (Hugo)-[:ACTED_IN {
  roles:[
    'Bill Smoke',
    'Haskell Moore',
    'Tadeusz Kesselring',
    'Nurse Noakes',
    'Boardman Mephi',
    'Old Georgie'
  ]
}]->(CloudAtlas)
MERGE (HalleB)-[:ACTED_IN {
  roles:['Luisa Rey', 'Jocasta Ayrs', 'Ovid', 'Meronym']
}]->(CloudAtlas)
MERGE (JimB)-[:ACTED_IN {
  roles:['Vyvyan Ayrs', 'Captain Molyneux', 'Timothy Cavendish']
}]->(CloudAtlas)
MERGE (TomT)-[:DIRECTED]->(CloudAtlas)
MERGE (LillyW)-[:DIRECTED]->(CloudAtlas)
MERGE (LanaW)-[:DIRECTED]->(CloudAtlas)
```

```
MERGE (DavidMitchell)-[:WROTE]->(CloudAtlas)
MERGE (StefanArndt)-[:PRODUCED]->(CloudAtlas);

MERGE (TheDaVinciCode:Movie {title:'The Da Vinci Code'}) ON CREATE SET
TheDaVinciCode.released=2006, TheDaVinciCode.tagline='Break The Codes'

MERGE (TomH:Person {name:'Tom Hanks'}) ON CREATE SET TomH.born=1956
MERGE (IanM:Person {name:'Ian McKellen'}) ON CREATE SET IanM.born=1939
MERGE (AudreyT:Person {name:'Audrey Tautou'})
ON CREATE SET AudreyT.born=1976
MERGE (PaulB:Person {name:'Paul Bettany'}) ON CREATE SET PaulB.born=1971
MERGE (RonH:Person {name:'Ron Howard'}) ON CREATE SET RonH.born=1954

MERGE (TomH)-[:ACTED_IN {roles:['Dr. Robert Langdon']}]->(TheDaVinciCode)
MERGE (IanM)-[:ACTED_IN {roles:['Sir Leight Teabing']}]->(TheDaVinciCode)
MERGE (AudreyT)-[:ACTED_IN {roles:['Sophie Neveu']}]->(TheDaVinciCode)
MERGE (PaulB)-[:ACTED_IN {roles:['Silas']}]->(TheDaVinciCode)
MERGE (RonH)-[:DIRECTED]->(TheDaVinciCode);

MERGE (VforVendetta:Movie {title:'V for Vendetta'}) ON CREATE SET
VforVendetta.released=2006, VforVendetta.tagline='Freedom! Forever!'

MERGE (Hugo:Person {name:'Hugo Weaving'}) ON CREATE SET Hugo.born=1960
MERGE (NatalieP:Person {name:'Natalie Portman'})
ON CREATE SET NatalieP.born=1981
MERGE (StephenR:Person {name:'Stephen Rea'})
ON CREATE SET StephenR.born=1946
MERGE (JohnH:Person {name:'John Hurt'}) ON CREATE SET JohnH.born=1940
MERGE (BenM:Person {name:'Ben Miles'}) ON CREATE SET BenM.born=1967
MERGE (LillyW:Person {name:'Lilly Wachowski'})
ON CREATE SET LillyW.born=1967
MERGE (LanaW:Person {name:'Lana Wachowski'}) ON CREATE SET LanaW.born=1965
MERGE (JamesM:Person {name:'James Marshall'}) ON CREATE SET JamesM.born=1967
MERGE (JoelS:Person {name:'Joel Silver'}) ON CREATE SET JoelS.born=1952

MERGE (Hugo)-[:ACTED_IN {roles:['V']}]->(VforVendetta)
MERGE (NatalieP)-[:ACTED_IN {roles:['Evey Hammond']}]->(VforVendetta)
MERGE (StephenR)-[:ACTED_IN {roles:['Eric Finch']}]->(VforVendetta)
MERGE (JohnH)-[:ACTED_IN {
  roles:['High Chancellor Adam Sutler']
}]->(VforVendetta)
MERGE (BenM)-[:ACTED_IN {roles:['Dascomb']}]->(VforVendetta)
MERGE (JamesM)-[:DIRECTED]->(VforVendetta)
MERGE (LillyW)-[:PRODUCED]->(VforVendetta)
MERGE (LanaW)-[:PRODUCED]->(VforVendetta)
MERGE (JoelS)-[:PRODUCED]->(VforVendetta)
MERGE (LillyW)-[:WROTE]->(VforVendetta)
MERGE (LanaW)-[:WROTE]->(VforVendetta);

MERGE (SpeedRacer:Movie {title:'Speed Racer'}) ON CREATE SET
SpeedRacer.released=2008, SpeedRacer.tagline='Speed has no limits'

MERGE (EmileH:Person {name:'Emile Hirsch'}) ON CREATE SET EmileH.born=1985
MERGE (JohnG:Person {name:'John Goodman'}) ON CREATE SET JohnG.born=1960
MERGE (SusanS:Person {name:'Susan Sarandon'}) ON CREATE SET SusanS.born=1946
```

```
MERGE (MatthewF:Person {name:'Matthew Fox'})
ON CREATE SET MatthewF.born=1966
MERGE (ChristinaR:Person {name:'Christina Ricci'})
ON CREATE SET ChristinaR.born=1980
MERGE (Rain:Person {name:'Rain'}) ON CREATE SET Rain.born=1982
MERGE (BenM:Person {name:'Ben Miles'}) ON CREATE SET BenM.born=1967
MERGE (LillyW:Person {name:'Lilly Wachowski'})
ON CREATE SET LillyW.born=1967
MERGE (LanaW:Person {name:'Lana Wachowski'}) ON CREATE SET LanaW.born=1965
MERGE (JoelS:Person {name:'Joel Silver'}) ON CREATE SET JoelS.born=1952

MERGE (EmileH)-[:ACTED_IN {roles:['Speed Racer']}]->(SpeedRacer)
MERGE (JohnG)-[:ACTED_IN {roles:['Pops']}]->(SpeedRacer)
MERGE (SusanS)-[:ACTED_IN {roles:['Mom']}]->(SpeedRacer)
MERGE (MatthewF)-[:ACTED_IN {roles:['Racer X']}]->(SpeedRacer)
MERGE (ChristinaR)-[:ACTED_IN {roles:['Trixie']}]->(SpeedRacer)
MERGE (Rain)-[:ACTED_IN {roles:['Taejo Togokahn']}]->(SpeedRacer)
MERGE (BenM)-[:ACTED_IN {roles:['Cass Jones']}]->(SpeedRacer)
MERGE (LillyW)-[:DIRECTED]->(SpeedRacer)
MERGE (LanaW)-[:DIRECTED]->(SpeedRacer)
MERGE (LillyW)-[:WROTE]->(SpeedRacer)
MERGE (LanaW)-[:WROTE]->(SpeedRacer)
MERGE (JoelS)-[:PRODUCED]->(SpeedRacer);

MERGE (NinjaAssassin:Movie {title:'Ninja Assassin'}) ON CREATE SET
 NinjaAssassin.released=2009,
 NinjaAssassin.tagline='Prepare to enter a secret world of assassins'

MERGE (NaomieH:Person {name:'Naomie Harris'})
MERGE (Rain:Person {name:'Rain'}) ON CREATE SET Rain.born=1982
MERGE (BenM:Person {name:'Ben Miles'}) ON CREATE SET BenM.born=1967
MERGE (LillyW:Person {name:'Lilly Wachowski'})
ON CREATE SET LillyW.born=1967
MERGE (LanaW:Person {name:'Lana Wachowski'}) ON CREATE SET LanaW.born=1965
MERGE (RickY:Person {name:'Rick Yune'}) ON CREATE SET RickY.born=1971
MERGE (JamesM:Person {name:'James Marshall'}) ON CREATE SET JamesM.born=1967
MERGE (JoelS:Person {name:'Joel Silver'}) ON CREATE SET JoelS.born=1952

MERGE (Rain)-[:ACTED_IN {roles:['Raizo']}]->(NinjaAssassin)
MERGE (NaomieH)-[:ACTED_IN {roles:['Mika Coretti']}]->(NinjaAssassin)
MERGE (RickY)-[:ACTED_IN {roles:['Takeshi']}]->(NinjaAssassin)
MERGE (BenM)-[:ACTED_IN {roles:['Ryan Maslow']}]->(NinjaAssassin)
MERGE (JamesM)-[:DIRECTED]->(NinjaAssassin)
MERGE (LillyW)-[:PRODUCED]->(NinjaAssassin)
MERGE (LanaW)-[:PRODUCED]->(NinjaAssassin)
MERGE (JoelS)-[:PRODUCED]->(NinjaAssassin);

MERGE (TheGreenMile:Movie {title:'The Green Mile'}) ON CREATE SET
TheGreenMile.released=1999,
TheGreenMile.tagline='Walk a mile you\'ll never forget.'

MERGE (TomH:Person {name:'Tom Hanks'}) ON CREATE SET TomH.born=1956
MERGE (JamesC:Person {name:'James Cromwell'}) ON CREATE SET JamesC.born=1940
MERGE (BonnieH:Person {name:'Bonnie Hunt'}) ON CREATE SET BonnieH.born=1961
MERGE (MichaelD:Person {name:'Michael Clarke Duncan'})
```

```
ON CREATE SET MichaelD.born=1957
MERGE (DavidM:Person {name:'David Morse'}) ON CREATE SET DavidM.born=1953
MERGE (SamR:Person {name:'Sam Rockwell'}) ON CREATE SET SamR.born=1968
MERGE (GaryS:Person {name:'Gary Sinise'}) ON CREATE SET GaryS.born=1955
MERGE (PatriciaC:Person {name:'Patricia Clarkson'})
ON CREATE SET PatriciaC.born=1959
MERGE (FrankD:Person {name:'Frank Darabont'}) ON CREATE SET FrankD.born=1959

MERGE (TomH)-[:ACTED_IN {roles:['Paul Edgecomb']}]->(TheGreenMile)
MERGE (MichaelD)-[:ACTED_IN {roles:['John Coffey']}]->(TheGreenMile)
MERGE (DavidM)-[:ACTED_IN {
  roles:['Brutus "Brutal" Howell']
}]->(TheGreenMile)
MERGE (BonnieH)-[:ACTED_IN {roles:['Jan Edgecomb']}]->(TheGreenMile)
MERGE (JamesC)-[:ACTED_IN {roles:['Warden Hal Moores']}]->(TheGreenMile)
MERGE (SamR)-[:ACTED_IN {roles:['"Wild Bill" Wharton']}]->(TheGreenMile)
MERGE (GaryS)-[:ACTED_IN {roles:['Burt Hammersmith']}]->(TheGreenMile)
MERGE (PatriciaC)-[:ACTED_IN {roles:['Melinda Moores']}]->(TheGreenMile)
MERGE (FrankD)-[:DIRECTED]->(TheGreenMile);

MERGE (FrostNixon:Movie {title:'Frost/Nixon'}) ON CREATE SET
FrostNixon.released=2008,
FrostNixon.tagline='400 million people were waiting for the truth.'

MERGE (FrankL:Person {name:'Frank Langella'}) ON CREATE SET FrankL.born=1938
MERGE (MichaelS:Person {name:'Michael Sheen'})
ON CREATE SET MichaelS.born=1969
MERGE (OliverP:Person {name:'Oliver Platt'}) ON CREATE SET OliverP.born=1960
MERGE (KevinB:Person {name:'Kevin Bacon'}) ON CREATE SET KevinB.born=1958
MERGE (SamR:Person {name:'Sam Rockwell'}) ON CREATE SET SamR.born=1968
MERGE (RonH:Person {name:'Ron Howard'}) ON CREATE SET RonH.born=1954

MERGE (FrankL)-[:ACTED_IN {roles:['Richard Nixon']}]->(FrostNixon)
MERGE (MichaelS)-[:ACTED_IN {roles:['David Frost']}]->(FrostNixon)
MERGE (KevinB)-[:ACTED_IN {roles:['Jack Brennan']}]->(FrostNixon)
MERGE (OliverP)-[:ACTED_IN {roles:['Bob Zelnick']}]->(FrostNixon)
MERGE (SamR)-[:ACTED_IN {roles:['James Reston, Jr.']}]->(FrostNixon)
MERGE (RonH)-[:DIRECTED]->(FrostNixon);

MERGE (Hoffa:Movie {title:'Hoffa'}) ON CREATE SET
Hoffa.released=1992, Hoffa.tagline='He didn\'t want law. He wanted justice.'

MERGE (DannyD:Person {name:'Danny DeVito'}) ON CREATE SET DannyD.born=1944
MERGE (JohnR:Person {name:'John C. Reilly'}) ON CREATE SET JohnR.born=1965
MERGE (JackN:Person {name:'Jack Nicholson'}) ON CREATE SET JackN.born=1937
MERGE (JTW:Person {name:'J.T. Walsh'}) ON CREATE SET JTW.born=1943

MERGE (JackN)-[:ACTED_IN {roles:['Hoffa']}]->(Hoffa)
MERGE (DannyD)-[:ACTED_IN {roles:['Robert "Bobby" Ciaro']}]->(Hoffa)
MERGE (JTW)-[:ACTED_IN {roles:['Frank Fitzsimmons']}]->(Hoffa)
MERGE (JohnR)-[:ACTED_IN {roles:['Peter "Pete" Connelly']}]->(Hoffa)
MERGE (DannyD)-[:DIRECTED]->(Hoffa);

MERGE (Apollo13:Movie {title:'Apollo 13'}) ON CREATE SET
Apollo13.released=1995, Apollo13.tagline='Houston, we have a problem.'
```

```
MERGE (TomH:Person {name:'Tom Hanks'}) ON CREATE SET TomH.born=1956
MERGE (EdH:Person {name:'Ed Harris'}) ON CREATE SET EdH.born=1950
MERGE (BillPax:Person {name:'Bill Paxton'}) ON CREATE SET BillPax.born=1955
MERGE (KevinB:Person {name:'Kevin Bacon'}) ON CREATE SET KevinB.born=1958
MERGE (GaryS:Person {name:'Gary Sinise'}) ON CREATE SET GaryS.born=1955
MERGE (RonH:Person {name:'Ron Howard'}) ON CREATE SET RonH.born=1954

MERGE (TomH)-[:ACTED_IN {roles:['Jim Lovell']}]->(Apollo13)
MERGE (KevinB)-[:ACTED_IN {roles:['Jack Swigert']}]->(Apollo13)
MERGE (EdH)-[:ACTED_IN {roles:['Gene Kranz']}]->(Apollo13)
MERGE (BillPax)-[:ACTED_IN {roles:['Fred Haise']}]->(Apollo13)
MERGE (GaryS)-[:ACTED_IN {roles:['Ken Mattingly']}]->(Apollo13)
MERGE (RonH)-[:DIRECTED]->(Apollo13);

MERGE (Twister:Movie {title:'Twister'}) ON CREATE SET
Twister.released=1996, Twister.tagline='Don\'t Breathe. Don\'t Look Back.'

MERGE (PhilipH:Person {name:'Philip Seymour Hoffman'})
ON CREATE SET PhilipH.born=1967
MERGE (JanB:Person {name:'Jan de Bont'}) ON CREATE SET JanB.born=1943
MERGE (BillPax:Person {name:'Bill Paxton'}) ON CREATE SET BillPax.born=1955
MERGE (HelenH:Person {name:'Helen Hunt'}) ON CREATE SET HelenH.born=1963
MERGE (ZachG:Person {name:'Zach Grenier'}) ON CREATE SET ZachG.born=1954

MERGE (BillPax)-[:ACTED_IN {roles:['Bill Harding']}]->(Twister)
MERGE (HelenH)-[:ACTED_IN {roles:['Dr. Jo Harding']}]->(Twister)
MERGE (ZachG)-[:ACTED_IN {roles:['Eddie']}]->(Twister)
MERGE (PhilipH)-[:ACTED_IN {roles:['Dustin "Dusty" Davis']}]->(Twister)
MERGE (JanB)-[:DIRECTED]->(Twister);

MERGE (CastAway:Movie {title:'Cast Away'}) ON CREATE SET
CastAway.released=2000,
CastAway.tagline='At the edge of the world, his journey begins.'

MERGE (TomH:Person {name:'Tom Hanks'}) ON CREATE SET TomH.born=1956
MERGE (HelenH:Person {name:'Helen Hunt'}) ON CREATE SET HelenH.born=1963
MERGE (RobertZ:Person {name:'Robert Zemeckis'})
ON CREATE SET RobertZ.born=1951

MERGE (TomH)-[:ACTED_IN {roles:['Chuck Noland']}]->(CastAway)
MERGE (HelenH)-[:ACTED_IN {roles:['Kelly Frears']}]->(CastAway)
MERGE (RobertZ)-[:DIRECTED]->(CastAway);

MERGE (OneFlewOvertheCuckoosNest:Movie {
  title:'One Flew Over the Cuckoo\'s Nest'
}) ON CREATE SET
OneFlewOvertheCuckoosNest.released=1975,
OneFlewOvertheCuckoosNest.tagline='If he\'s crazy, what does that make you?'

MERGE (MilosF:Person {name:'Milos Forman'}) ON CREATE SET MilosF.born=1932
MERGE (JackN:Person {name:'Jack Nicholson'}) ON CREATE SET JackN.born=1937
MERGE (DannyD:Person {name:'Danny DeVito'}) ON CREATE SET DannyD.born=1944

MERGE (JackN)-[:ACTED_IN {
  roles:['Randle McMurphy']
```

```
}]->(OneFlewOvertheCuckoosNest)
MERGE (DannyD)-[:ACTED_IN {roles:['Martini']}]->(OneFlewOvertheCuckoosNest)
MERGE (MilosF)-[:DIRECTED]->(OneFlewOvertheCuckoosNest);

MERGE (SomethingsGottaGive:Movie {title:'Something\'s Gotta Give'})
ON CREATE SET SomethingsGottaGive.released=2003

MERGE (JackN:Person {name:'Jack Nicholson'}) ON CREATE SET JackN.born=1937
MERGE (DianeK:Person {name:'Diane Keaton'}) ON CREATE SET DianeK.born=1946
MERGE (NancyM:Person {name:'Nancy Meyers'}) ON CREATE SET NancyM.born=1949
MERGE (Keanu:Person {name:'Keanu Reeves'}) ON CREATE SET Keanu.born=1964

MERGE (JackN)-[:ACTED_IN {roles:['Harry Sanborn']}]->(SomethingsGottaGive)
MERGE (DianeK)-[:ACTED_IN {roles:['Erica Barry']}]->(SomethingsGottaGive)
MERGE (Keanu)-[:ACTED_IN {roles:['Julian Mercer']}]->(SomethingsGottaGive)
MERGE (NancyM)-[:DIRECTED]->(SomethingsGottaGive)
MERGE (NancyM)-[:PRODUCED]->(SomethingsGottaGive)
MERGE (NancyM)-[:WROTE]->(SomethingsGottaGive);

MERGE (BicentennialMan:Movie {title:'Bicentennial Man'}) ON CREATE SET
BicentennialMan.released=1999,
BicentennialMan.tagline='One robot\'s 200 year journey to become an ordinary
➥ man.'

MERGE (ChrisC:Person {name:'Chris Columbus'}) ON CREATE SET ChrisC.born=1958
MERGE (Robin:Person {name:'Robin Williams'}) ON CREATE SET Robin.born=1951
MERGE (OliverP:Person {name:'Oliver Platt'}) ON CREATE SET OliverP.born=1960

MERGE (Robin)-[:ACTED_IN {roles:['Andrew Marin']}]->(BicentennialMan)
MERGE (OliverP)-[:ACTED_IN {roles:['Rupert Burns']}]->(BicentennialMan)
MERGE (ChrisC)-[:DIRECTED]->(BicentennialMan);

MERGE (CharlieWilsonsWar:Movie {title:'Charlie Wilson\'s War'})
ON CREATE SET CharlieWilsonsWar.released=2007,
CharlieWilsonsWar.tagline='A stiff drink. A little mascara. A lot of nerve.
➥ Who said they couldn\'t bring down the Soviet empire.'

MERGE (TomH:Person {name:'Tom Hanks'}) ON CREATE SET TomH.born=1956
MERGE (PhilipH:Person {name:'Philip Seymour Hoffman'})
ON CREATE SET PhilipH.born=1967
MERGE (JuliaR:Person {name:'Julia Roberts'}) ON CREATE SET JuliaR.born=1967
MERGE (MikeN:Person {name:'Mike Nichols'}) ON CREATE SET MikeN.born=1931

MERGE (TomH)-[:ACTED_IN {
  roles:['Rep. Charlie Wilson']
}]->(CharlieWilsonsWar)
MERGE (JuliaR)-[:ACTED_IN {roles:['Joanne Herring']}]->(CharlieWilsonsWar)
MERGE (PhilipH)-[:ACTED_IN {roles:['Gust Avrakotos']}]->(CharlieWilsonsWar)
MERGE (MikeN)-[:DIRECTED]->(CharlieWilsonsWar);

MERGE (ThePolarExpress:Movie {title:'The Polar Express'}) ON CREATE SET
ThePolarExpress.released=2004,
ThePolarExpress.tagline='This Holiday Season... Believe'
```

```
MERGE (TomH:Person {name:'Tom Hanks'}) ON CREATE SET TomH.born=1956
MERGE (RobertZ:Person {name:'Robert Zemeckis'})
ON CREATE SET RobertZ.born=1951

MERGE (TomH)-[:ACTED_IN {
  roles:[
    'Hero Boy',
    'Father',
    'Conductor',
    'Hobo',
    'Scrooge',
    'Santa Claus'
  ]
}]->(ThePolarExpress)
MERGE (RobertZ)-[:DIRECTED]->(ThePolarExpress);

MERGE (ALeagueofTheirOwn:Movie {title:'A League of Their Own'})
ON CREATE SET ALeagueofTheirOwn.released=1992,
ALeagueofTheirOwn.tagline='Once in a lifetime you get a chance to do
➥ something different.'

MERGE (TomH:Person {name:'Tom Hanks'}) ON CREATE SET TomH.born=1956
MERGE (Madonna:Person {name:'Madonna'}) ON CREATE SET Madonna.born=1954
MERGE (GeenaD:Person {name:'Geena Davis'}) ON CREATE SET GeenaD.born=1956
MERGE (LoriP:Person {name:'Lori Petty'}) ON CREATE SET LoriP.born=1963
MERGE (PennyM:Person {name:'Penny Marshall'}) ON CREATE SET PennyM.born=1943
MERGE (RosieO:Person {name:'Rosie O\'Donnell'})
ON CREATE SET RosieO.born=1962
MERGE (BillPax:Person {name:'Bill Paxton'}) ON CREATE SET BillPax.born=1955

MERGE (TomH)-[:ACTED_IN {roles:['Jimmy Dugan']}]->(ALeagueofTheirOwn)
MERGE (GeenaD)-[:ACTED_IN {roles:['Dottie Hinson']}]->(ALeagueofTheirOwn)
MERGE (LoriP)-[:ACTED_IN {roles:['Kit Keller']}]->(ALeagueofTheirOwn)
MERGE (RosieO)-[:ACTED_IN {roles:['Doris Murphy']}]->(ALeagueofTheirOwn)
MERGE (Madonna)-[:ACTED_IN {
  roles:['"All the Way" Mae Mordabito']
}]->(ALeagueofTheirOwn)
MERGE (BillPax)-[:ACTED_IN {roles:['Bob Hinson']}]->(ALeagueofTheirOwn)
MERGE (PennyM)-[:DIRECTED]->(ALeagueofTheirOwn);


MATCH (CloudAtlas:Movie {title:'Cloud Atlas'})
MATCH (TheReplacements:Movie {title:'The Replacements'})
MATCH (Unforgiven:Movie {title:'Unforgiven'})
MATCH (TheBirdcage:Movie {title:'The Birdcage'})
MATCH (TheDaVinciCode:Movie {title:'The Da Vinci Code'})
MATCH (JerryMaguire:Movie {title:'Jerry Maguire'})

MERGE (PaulBlythe:Person {name:'Paul Blythe'})
MERGE (AngelaScope:Person {name:'Angela Scope'})
MERGE (JessicaThompson:Person {name:'Jessica Thompson'})
MERGE (JamesThompson:Person {name:'James Thompson'})
```

```
MERGE (JamesThompson)-[:FOLLOWS]->(JessicaThompson)
MERGE (AngelaScope)-[:FOLLOWS]->(JessicaThompson)
MERGE (PaulBlythe)-[:FOLLOWS]->(AngelaScope)

MERGE (JessicaThompson)-[:REVIEWED {
  summary:'An amazing journey', rating:95
}]->(CloudAtlas)
MERGE (JessicaThompson)-[:REVIEWED {
  summary:'Silly, but fun', rating:65
}]->(TheReplacements)
MERGE (JamesThompson)-[:REVIEWED {
  summary:'The coolest football movie ever', rating:100
}]->(TheReplacements)
MERGE (AngelaScope)-[:REVIEWED {
  summary:'Pretty funny at times', rating:62
}]->(TheReplacements)
MERGE (JessicaThompson)-[:REVIEWED {
  summary:'Dark, but compelling', rating:85
}]->(Unforgiven)
MERGE (JessicaThompson)-[:REVIEWED {
  summary:"Slapstick redeemed only by the Robin Williams and Gene Hackman's
➥ stellar performances",
  rating:45
}]->(TheBirdcage)
MERGE (JessicaThompson)-[:REVIEWED {
  summary:'A solid romp', rating:68
}]->(TheDaVinciCode)
MERGE (JamesThompson)-[:REVIEWED {
  summary:'Fun, but a little far fetched', rating:65
}]->(TheDaVinciCode)
MERGE (JessicaThompson)-[:REVIEWED {
  summary:'You had me at Jerry', rating:9
2}]->(JerryMaguire);
```

references

Achiam, J. et al.; OpenAI. (2024). GPT-4 Technical Report. https://arxiv.org/abs/2303.08774.

Caudhuri, A. K. (2017). Einstein's Patents and Inventions. https://arxiv.org/abs/1709.00666.

Den Wins 4-1 (2025). https://www.nba.com/playoffs/2023/the-finals.

Deutsch, A. et al. (2022). Graph Pattern Matching in GQL and SQL/PGQ. In *Proceedings of the 2022 International Conference on Management of Data* (pp. 2246–2258). Association for Computing Machinery.

Doyle, R. (2023, December 28). What Selling the Dallas Mavericks Means for Mark Cuban and the Future of the Team. https://mng.bz/lZM8.

Gao, Luyu, Xueguang Ma, Jimmy Lin, and Jamie Callan. (2022). Precise Zero-Shot Dense Retrieval without Relevance Labels. https://arxiv.org/abs/2212.10496.

GQL Standards Committee. (n.d.). Retrieved August 30, 2023, https://www.gqlstandards.org/home/.

Hendrycks, Dan, Collin Burns, Anya Chen, and Sencer Ball. (2021). CUAD: An Expert-Annotated NLP Dataset for Legal Contract Review. https://arxiv.org/abs/2103.06268.

Lewis, Patrick et al. (2021). Retrieval-Augmented Generation for Knowledge-Intensive NLP Tasks. https://arxiv.org/abs/2005.11401.

Neumeister, Larry. (2023, June 8). Lawyers Blame ChatGPT for Tricking Them into Citing Bogus Case Law. https://mng.bz/Bzd8.

openCypher Implementers Group. (n.d.). Retrieved August 30, 2023, https://opencypher.org/projects/.

Ovadia, O., M. Brief, M. Mishaeli, and O. Elisha. (2023). Fine-Tuning or Retrieval? Comparing Knowledge Injection in LLMs. https://arxiv.org/abs/2312.05934.

Tian, K., E. Mitchell, H. Yao, C.D. Manning, and C. Finn. (2023). Fine-Tuning Language Models for Factuality. https://arxiv.org/abs/2311.08401.

Vaswani, A. et al. (2017). Attention Is All You Need. https://arxiv.org/abs/1706.03762.

Yao, S. et al. (2023). ReAct: Synergizing Reasoning and Acting in Language Models https://arxiv.org/abs/2210.03629.

Zheng, H. S. et al. (2023). Take a Step Back: Evoking Reasoning via Abstraction in Large Language Models. https://arxiv.org/abs/2310.06117.

index

A

B

C

D

E

F